The Sol Plaatje European Union Poetry Anthology

Vol IX

The Sol Plaatje European Union Poetry Anthology

Volume IX

Selected by Mongane Wally Serote, Goodenough Mashego, Pieter Odendaal, Innocentia Mhlambi, Neo Sehlahla, Sponono Mahlangu, Rustum Kozain & Athol Williams

The views and opinions expressed in this publication are not necessarily those of the funder.

First published by Jacana Media (Pty) Ltd in 2019

10 Orange Street
Sunnyside
Auckland Park 2092
South Africa
+2711 628 3200
www.jacana.co.za

© Individual contributers, 2019

All rights reserved.

ISBN 978-1-4314-2954-7

Cover photograph © Alexia Webster (www.alexiawebster.com)
Set in Ehrhardt 11/13pt
Printed and bound by Creda Communications
Job no. 003636

See a complete list of Jacana titles at www.jacana.co.za

CONTENTS

Foreword *Dr Mongane Wally Serote* xi
Message from the Sponsor *EU Ambassaodor to South Africa,
Dr Riina Kionka* xxi

UBUMAMA, *Zukiswa Muriel Adonis* 1
MOTHERHOOD,
   an English translation by Innocentia Mhlambi 3
HAWKERS, *Jayne Bauling* 6
NOT ONE OF US, *Jayne Bauling* 7
SIXTH SENSE ON THE LINGA LINGA, *Michèle Betty* 8
CALLING HOME, *Marike Beyers* 9
SUNDAY, *Marike Beyers* 10
WHAT'S IN A WORD, *Nicola Brighton* 11
NIGHT WALK, *Christine Coates* 12
MPA MOSWENG, *Sannah Cujane* 13
TEENAGE PREGNANCY, *an English translation
   by Goodeneough Mashego* 14
REVOLUTION, *Luthando Dlamini* 16
THE TONER ON THE PRINTER HAS RUN OUT,
   Chris Ellis 17
DIT LYK ALWEE NA REËN, *Kimberly Flanagan* 18
LOOKS LIKE RAIN AGAIN, *an English translation
   by Pieter Odendaal* 19
IKHUTSE LEPANTSOLA, *Tshepo Gaerupe* 20
REST PANTSULA, *an English translation
   by Goodeneough Mashego* 22
AGAIN, *Dawn Garisch* 24

OLD BLOOD, *Sarah Godsell* 25
THE POLITICS OF A WALL, *Vernon R.L. Head* 26
TIKO RA LOVA, *Miyelani Anthonia Hlungwani* 28
OUR COUNTRY IS DYING, *an English translation
by Neo Sehlahla* 30
SOLOMON TSHEKISHO PLAATJE,
Miyelani Anthonia Hlungwani 32
SOLOMON TSHEKISHO PLAATJE,
an English translation by Neo Sehlahla 34
MUDYONDZISI WA LUNYA,
Mashimbye Owners Hluvukani 36
A TEACHER WHO IS A WRONGDOER,
an English translation by Neo Sehlahla 37
RAIN BULL, *Alice Inggs* 38
UBUQAQAWULI BUKA PLAATJE, *Siphelele Khaphetshu* ... 40
THE GLORY OF PLAATJE, *an English translation
by Innocentia Mhlambi* 43
UNOMKHUBULWANE WAMI, *Zandile Khumalo* 46
MY NOMKHUBULWANE, *an English translation
by Innocentia Mhlambi* 48
NDI NGAVHA NDO KHAKHA, *Zamokwakhe Kumbe* 51
I MIGHT HAVE BEEN WRONG, *an English translation
by Neo Sehlahla* 52
DISPATCH FROM WARD C, *Sarah Lubala* 54
ILLING ROAD, *Zamokuhle Madinana* 57
INKOLO YAKWANTU, *Afikile Madiya* 58
THE NATIVE BELIEF, *an English translation
by Innocentia Mhlambi* 59
POPPY WELATH, *Clare Manicom* 61
NITHI NGIYO LE IKULULEKO?, *Ayanda Masango* 62

ARE YOU SAYING THIS IS THE FREEDOM?, *an English translation by Sponono Mahlangu* 63

NIZOKULISA NINI?, *Bongani Masilela* 64

WHEN ARE YOU GOING TO STOP, *an English translation by Bongani Masilela* 66

DIVINERS, *Linda Masilela* 68

HO SENYEHILE KAE?, *Aaron Mpho Masowa* 71

WHERE DID WE GO WRONG?, *an English translation by Innocentia Mhlambi* 75

FOR THE BROKEN BOY, *Tebogo Matshana* 79

SASIPHI NA ISAZELA?, *Mzoli Mavimbela*................ 80

WHERE WAS HIS/HER CONSCIENCE?, *an English translation by Innocentia Mhlambi*............... 81

CARNIVORE, *Jeannie Wallace McKeown* 83

DANCE WITH US IN LAVENDER HILL, MY CHILD, *Frank Meintjies*....................................... 84

AUTUMN, *Janine Milne* 85

MOTHER OF KNIVES, *Janine Milne* 86

BOTSANA, *Matete Motsoaledi* 88

BEAUTY, *an English translation by Goodeneough Mashego*...... 90

MY MOTHER TONGUE, *Zimkitha Mpatheni* 92

NGIYIMPUMPUTHE, *Kwanza Ndlangisa* 93

I AM BLIND, *an English translation by Innocentia Mhlambi* 95

NGIYINGXENYE YOMOYA, *Kwanza Ndlangisa*........... 98

I AM PART OF THE WIND, *an English translation by Innocentia Mhlambi*............................... 100

KWANGA, *Kwanza Ndlangisa*.......................... 102

IT IS AS THOUGH, *an English translation by Innocentia Mhlambi*............................... 104

IQHIYA, *Abongile Njamela*............................. 106

THE DOEK, *an English translation
by Innocentia Mhlambi* 109

CHRISTMAS LUNCH, *Zukisani Nongogo* 112

THE PERCUSSIONIST, *Fumane Ntlhabane* 114

LETTER TO THE FATHER, *Thulani Ntisana* 115

BAMBATHA, *Sihle Ntuli*............................ 117

BAMBATHA, *an English translation by Innocentia Mhlambi* ... 119

NDWANGU, *Sihle Ntuli* 120

GARMENT, *an English translation by by Innocentia Mhlambi* .. 123

TAKUTSHEDZA IWE RAMAPHOSA,
Mushayathoni Nwovhe 126

STAND UP RAMAPHOSA, *an English translation
by Neo Sehlahla* 129

ZINGCE M-AFRIKA, *Zukiswa Mercy Pakama* 133

TAKE PRIDE IN YOURSELF, AFRICAN,
an English translation by Innocentia Mhlambi...... 135

SESWANTŠHO SA GAGO, *Kagiso Mosima Phakane* 137

YOUR PICTURE, *an English translation
by Goodeneough Mashego* 139

THE MARK OF A FREE AND FAIR ELECTION,
Catherine Pritchard.............................. 141

DIE KRUIEMAN, *Wesley Roodt* 144

THE HERBALIST, *an English translation
by Pieter Odendaal* 145

O BE O LE KAE?, *Moses Seletisha*.................. 146

WHERE WERE YOU?, *an English translation
by Goodeneough Mashego* 150

EMATYOTYOMBENI, *Siwaphiwe Fortune Shweni* 154

AT THE INFORMAL SETTLEMENTS, *an English translation
by Innocentia Mhlambi*156 ....

DEPRESSIVE EPISODES, *Caitlin Spring* 158

OVER THE LINE, *Caitlin Spring* 160
SPOOKASEM, *Elodi Troskie* 161
CANDYFLOSS, *an English translation by Pieter Odendaal* 163
MMILENG WA HILLBROW, *Thabang Tsolo* 165
ON A HILLBROW STREET, *an English translation
by Goodeneough Mashego* 167
LUFA SIJONGILE!, *Athini Watu* 169
IT DIES IN OUR WATCH, *an English translation
by Innocentia Mhlambi* 172
LESSONS, *Flow Wellington* 175
MY OUPA'S WATCH, *Stephanie Williams* 177
SEA, BOY, *Beatrice Willoughby* 178
ON THE EDGE OF DARKNESS, *Fiona Zerbst* 180
DISMANTLING FRANKENSTEIN'S DAUGHTER,
Thandiwe Zhanje................................. 181

Biographies... 182
What is the European Union?........................ 199

FOREWORD

What is poetry?

Is it an aesthetic expression? Is it a profound or simple social comment informed by a subject, which the poet feels must be expressed – and expresses no matter the result or consequence? Is it a profound or simple political comment, a view which has bewildered the poet? Is it an utterance of beauty or gloom or ugliness?

What is poetry?

Is it an expression of deeply felt emotions or just a form of writing with rhyme and rhythm? Is poetry words, words and words of emotion, aesthetics, packed in a certain form like a short or long queue expressing or seeking to explore or express a matter which the heart or the mind seeks to pour out?

The reality here is that, it is 2019, a year that, continuing from where other years kept whispering: '… Something is wrong in the land…'. The harsh realities of our country – South Africa – are being revealed. As ominous as that may sound, once more the poets, from different parts of our country, across the diverse spectrum of who we are as a people have put pen on paper. The writing is on the wall now. It has been for a while.

And so, we must ask a different question now. How does the nation relate to the poets? What must the poets do to reach out to the nation? How must the nation listen, get closer, and know what the poets do and why they say the things they say? How do the poets become the feel of the nation?

In other words, do the poets listen to the nation, does the nation listen to the poets, and if this symbiotic relation were a reality, how would it impact on the quality of the poets, and how would it impact on the quality of life of the nation?

The body of the collective poetic expression in this collection, which almost all the poets of our land search for and express, seeks to create and cement the seamless relationship between the creative community of our nation, with all the communities in the nation.

To those who are not parents distinctively, but have parentism ... carry on ... I encourage you.

To those who have miscarriages trying motherhood ... do not give up on God.

To those who give up their bodies to carry for their sister's, their cousins, friends and those they have never seen because of their love for motherhood ... you are right, you are kind.

To those who say, 'I gave birth to children, and they are nothing like me', it's alright when it is well with Him ... decisions are His.

To those without a conscious love of motherhood, transacting other people's children ... this day is coming to you.

To those who are not mentally stable, but when your minds come back and you are reminded that you are somebody's mother ... stay in hope. God is the helper.

To those who had a second of motherhood, a minute, an hour, a day, a week, a month, a year... Then the happiness ended whilst enjoying ... find comfort.

Motherhood
Adonis M Zukiswa

In all obstacles that you have gone through, it was meant to be
and it is alright because you were the chosen ones.
He has not forsaken you but it is then that you are closer to Him.
This too shall pass...
Keep quiet and know ... He is God.
In everything know that you are loved... be strong...
(an English translation by Innocentia Mhlambi)

Would the essence of this poem make the nation, us humans, to stop for a while and ask: what does this collective experience of womanhood mean? In other words, can the lines of this poem claim us, claim our consciousness? Can the lines after lines of the poem say to us, when all of these issues which this poem raises about women have been raised. They will formulate a collective national question in the minds of the individuals in our nation to ask: why is it so, and what can be done?

What must be done so that a means must be devised by the nation, to normalise the spiritual, mental and physical state of all the members of the nation, so that the health of the women of the nation is of quality? What must happen so that the inherent story line in each line of the poem can say that that story is a national collective responsibility? If so, would we ask: what must we do, so that we can go further to find out what must be done and do that? How do the arts, which are an underlining tapestry of culture, become the consciousness of a people?

One poem in this collection speaks with great care, in a

subtle manner about poverty, about being socially discriminated against, about being trapped in a cul-de-sac of life and the economy, and many other concur as others speak to the suffering of some citizens in communities, or shacks.

Dance With Us In Lavender Hill
Frank Meintjies

Do a dance with daddy
Before I shave and don my boots
Before I head out (leaning into the wind)
To pack & stack the orange & green
At the fruit & veggie stall…

…Dance with us, your ma and de
Be happy, little girl;
And, ja, we do know
There are thorns and petals
In our dusty little world.

Does the weight of all of these admonishing collective poetic voices, which are not only ably scripted in a variety of metaphors and techniques, but which claim the cultural diversity of our nation as our reality and wealth, shore up the drastic social, cultural and political crisis which they discern to be embedded in these communities? The poets come as a means to reach the national consciousness, to anchor on our being and ask: have you not read the writing on the wall yet?

Poem after poem after poem beckons and calls, asking the same question and seeking for an answer to the desperate national encounter. The poems portray the state of our country clearly, they articulate the fact that corruption is ravaging the means of the nation from lifting itself out of the morass of 'poverty', of being 'discriminated' against and being marginalised out of life by being 'unemployed'.

We have been here before as a nation; then we were organised in our Movement, we engaged in the anti-colonial and anti-apartheid mass, armed and underground struggles, and even laid our lives down to create a non-racial, non-sexist and democratic nation, which eventually, through votes, we let emerge.

The current reality of our country is that below the corruption which the poets so ably identify, hidden underneath are the '...conscious and deliberate...' acts which, while looting for individual gain, their conscious acts are to collapse the emerging non-racial, non-sexist and democratic nation and state. Before, we could clearly identify the regime that held fort for the apartheid system, but now, some of those who loot are among us, their acts complement and are complemented by some who are hiding their hand but who are in cahoots.

How must the poets, the singers, the creative communities, the cultural workers, find them and expose their deeds for what they are? What the poets clearly portray in this collection is not only what they discern from within the communities they come from or work in, but what they themselves experience by their closeness to the communities. What must the creative communities, the cultural workers, do together with the communities, do to write and read the writing on the wall correctly?

Their movement is under siege. The siege emanates from processes, which gnaw at the values of the movement of the people, which had successfully not only dislodged but also disintegrated the power of the apartheid state. What is that culture of the movement, what are those traditions, those values which those who hide behind corruption so skilfully distort and discredit?

The answers to those questions must be inherent in the aesthetics, metaphors, rhymes and rhythms of the poems, which ring and chime in the air now, at this hour of our history when the gains of the revolution of the people are being '...consciously and deliberately...' undermined. They will be. The beginning of that is the collective voice of these collected poems.

The evidence of that is in poem after poem after poem, all of which lament the fact that the centre is not holding – individuals, families, communities, the nation. Everything is disintegrating! It is as if soon, and after, there will be no stone, which can stand on another stone in communities.

At least some poems sing. Some asks us to a dance and others ask us to pray but because there is so much deep insecurity, simmering violence, protests, demonstrations and strikes, which at the least become defiant and unruly, these treasures of being become meaningless.

After all of that, the silence of the poems screams and asks: what must done? That question can only be attended to, it can only find answers if the political centre is holding, if the nation is anchored in hope and optimism, all of that reside in the history of this, our country-they shall be found and used. That resides among the people.

The herbalist
Wesley Roodt

...Among wrinkles he stores the

knowledge of ninety-five years
and in his hand he carries his kerrie
of wisdom.
And he speaks:

O, people who breed hate and disaster:
if you feed the darkness
it will only grow faster...

Wesley Roodt says here to come and experience what has tempered life, as a judge would justice, judge with mercy.

In a landscape which seems hostile, which gives the sense of emptiness bordering almost on death, the toothless 95-year-old herbalist sees the purple flower and the spoor of a jackal in the semi desert of the little Karoo; in other words, he perceives and sees signs of life and living right there in the nothingness. The herbalist knows, from having lived life that hope, optimism are not friends of fools.

What must be done – as the poets in this collection repeatedly remind us about the desperate poverty many live with – about the cruelty of being completely marginalised in society, because you cannot earn a living, about how like a cancer which refuses to shrivel and die, discrimination based on kinds of madness is justified to the extent that fences will be erected to bar human beings from crossing borders? That is an understatement, which that is why we, who fought for freedom cannot be xenophobic, a phenomena, which now seeks to take root in our country.

Sea, Boy
Beatrice Willoughby

Beatrice, why the contradictory refrain?

hey kira-kira boy,
hey surf boy,
boy with ocean lung:
Wooh, wooh!

with body of brown you boy the boat,
skin and salt - this is all you know:
warm water, sea snake, wild wave.

you have never sat at a ruler-scratched desk,
and i hope you do.
and i hope you never do

you have never felt the floor of a foreign land,
and i hope you do,
and i hope you never do.

i hope you learn to know the faces, spaces, traces of the world,
and i hope you never do.

oh kira-kira boy,
oh sea scrap boy,

i hope all you ever see is reef, deep and blue.

oh beach-bound boy;

go away boy,
stay boy

grow boy,
bide boy

you are free with the sea
you are jailed with the sea.

Are you being protective of the Sea Boy's joy, his innocence, his being playful, his skill and expertise and his mastering of the sea and its vastness? You are aware and it seems he is not, of its calmness and the inherent threat in it, which the Sea Boy dares?

The boy is like culture. He has learnt from history, which is why he is like culture. His history of practising to be on that soft mighty waters and be playful, joyful almost oblivious of any and every danger which may lurk by its side. There is an isiZulu saying which you evoke by this poem: *Sibindi u ya bolala, sibindi u ya philisa!* That is what the refrain in the poem is about. Certainly, there are many other meanings and interpretations one can derive from the poem and that is its strength, as playful as it is.

And so then, to the body of the collective poetry in this collection. The poets, like the poets must do, did not spare themselves. They threw in every skill, thought, emotion, knowledge and anger into everything, to put the proverbial writing on the wall.

They lament the political state and politics of our country. They cry about the social texture of our nation. They refuse to listen to any justification about why we are where we are socially, so torn apart. Bordering on despair, they do not hesitate to name and shame. They dare power. They are cynical. They are keenly aware of the variety of cruelty and violence in our nation. They dare and search for answers in belief systems, including spirituality and religion. Some search and probe the indigenous knowledge systems of this land.

There is a desperateness in the voices, metaphors and

speech of the poets and in the poems; as there is also scepticism, cynicism, anger and near violence against individuals, families, communities, the state, parliament. As the saying goes the poets are saying: "…the centre is not holding…"

The cohesion of our society, our nation has been undermined; it has been drastically compromised. In short, the symptoms are what the poets keep revisiting, which is what the collective poets speak of our country. The body of the collective poetic expression in this collection, which almost all the poets of our land search for and express, will soon bloom.

Is it counter-revolution that has gripped our nation, which seeks to disintegrate and destroy? If so, comrade poets: What must be done?

Mongane Wally Serote
August 2019

A MESSAGE FROM THE SPONSOR

Language is central to our existence. It is at the heart of our identity and forms one of the most important conduits between our ancestry, the present that we live in and our destiny. As a key constituent of culture, language shapes how we make sense of the world around us and, linked to this, how we chose to express ourselves. Language is vital to retaining our knowledge systems and cannot be underestimated in recording our experiences and emotions.

Our values are encoded in our respective languages. Who in South Africa does not know the Zulu word 'ubuntu' that not only is loosely translated to mean 'humanity', but that has a deeper and collectively aware meaning of 'I am because we are'.

Heritage Month this year was focused on all of South Africa's languages in an effort to preserve and promote the country's multitude of languages. Multilingualism is also a characteristic of the European Union with its 24 official languages.

I am delighted that the Sol Plaatje European Union poetry award and anthology, now in its ninth year, continues to be at the forefront of recognising all of South Africa's official languages. Poems that make the judges' long list are published in the official language they were submitted in. This is a remarkable project and I am delighted that the non-profit Jacana Literary Foundation has taken the lead in this initiative from its inception some ten years ago.

While I take this opportunity to heartily congratulate the three winners of this year's competition for their outstanding contributions to South Africa's rich tapestry of literary achievements, a special word of gratitude is owed to the many South African poets who submitted their work.

I salute the eminent panel of judges chaired by South Africa's deeply respected poet laureate, Mongane Wally Serote.

Thank you Jacana Media – recently acquired in a staff buy-out by two formidable voices in the local publishing industry, Bridget Impey and Maggie Davey – for your tireless support in realising an idea and turning it into an anthology ... a physical book ... that sells out year after year.

Dr Riina Kionka
EU Ambassador to South Africa

UBUMAMA
Xhosa

Kuni nozala, ndiyabulela.
Nisithwele kuloomazants'esinqe ngemincili mhlawumbe kwabanye ngesinyanzelo nangesingqala.
Kwabo babecwangcisile, iluvuyo nothando ukubumbeka kwethu... ndibeth'ingqongqo. Kwabo kwakumnandi kusisivumelwano mhla liqumfuzw'iqanda, kodwa walikheswa mhla wazithwala, waza waluthand'olosana... ndiyabulela.
Kwabo bophuk'ibele benziw'omama ngesinyanzelo...ngxesi.
Kuba nilunyamezel'olobizo nasithath'isigqibo nazingcama, nazivul'izandla zobubele zobuzali anazicekis'ezontsana... ndiyazithoba.
Kwabo bangazange babenakh'ukunyamezela, ngenxa yezidlwengu ezingenasazela, naziqhonf'izisu... andinigxeki.
Ngoku ninemivandedwa, niphathwa luvalo, nibizw'ababulali, namagqwirhakazi ngenxa yesisenzo... ndingubani ukuba ndigwebe... esona sihlobo nguYesu.
Kwabo banyamezeleyo kodwa ubukho bezontsana bunicingisa laamini imbi, izele bubumnyama nokuzicaphukela kuba kwatsalwa nina, bazithathela kulomhlab'ungezantsi. Nathath'isgqibo ukubanikezela kwikhaya leenkedama, kodwa kukho mini nimane nithuthuzela oo nodoli... umoy'unentumekelelo.
Kwabo basenza ngekratshi nangetshiki befun'ubuzali ngenkani, befun'ukuziphatha, kodwa anasitshintsha isiqibo senu... avulekil'amehlo.
Kwabo kwanyanzeleka phambi kwexesha ubumama ngenxa yobunkenenkene bamaqanda, naze nanqwala...ndiyanivuma.
Kwabo babefuna nje imbewu ukuze babe ngoomama... ndifunde-nto.

Kwabo bangengomama poqo kodwa benobuzali... qhubeka... ndiyakhuthaza.
Kwabo bawelwa zizisu bezama ubumama... ningamncam'uThixo.
Kwabo bancam'imizimba yabo bathwalel'odade babo, abazala babo, abahlobo babo kwakunye nabo bangazange baba bona ngenxa yothando lobumama... nilungile ninobubele. Kwabo bathi 'ndizel'abantwana baze bakreqa kum'... kulingile xa kulunge Kuye... izigqibo zeZakhe.
Kwabo bangesenayo inimba yobumama, benaniselana ngesizalo sabanye... lemin'iyeza nakuni.
Kwabo bazi 'umty'ungafikiy'eparafinini', kodwa mhla uthile zibuy'inqondo ukuba ungumama kazibani... hlalan'ethemben'uThixo engumncedi.
Kwabo babufuman'ubumama nje ngomzuzwana, ngomzuzu, ngeyure, ngosuku, ngeveki, ngenyanga, ngonyaka... Waze waqhawuk'ujing'abantwan'abedlala... thuthuzelekani.

Kuyo yonke lemeko nidlule kuyo bekufanelekile, kwaye kulungile kuba bekuchongwe nina. Akanishiyanga koko kukhona nisondeleyo Kuye.
Nale izakudlula...
Thulani nazi... unguThixo.
Kuko konke yazin'ukuba niyathandwa... yomelelani.

ZUKISWA MURIEL ADONIS

MOTHERHOOD

To you mothers, I thank you.
You have carried us in those lower parts of the abdomen with anticipation, maybe to others by force and cries.
To those who had been planned our coming to earth, our coming is joy and love... I'm beating on the metal sheet surface/praising you.
To those that had it nice whereby it was an agreement the day the egg was broken, but became exiled the day you were preganant, but loved this baby... I thank you.
To those who became pregnant and were made mothers by force... I'm sorry.
Because you have endured that calling and took a decision and devoted yourselves, opened your kind hands of parenthood and never hated those babies... I humble myself.
To those who could endure because of rapists with no guilt, and aborted your babies... I don't judge you.
Now you are depressed, afraid, called murderers and witches because of this act... who am I to judge... the ultimate friend is Jesus.
To those who are enduring the existence of those babies, which remind you of that bad day, filled with darkness and self-hate because you were pulled, and they helped themselves to your private parts.
You took a decision to give them to an orphanage home, but there are days when you comfort dolls... the spirit has condolences.
To those who made us with a grudge and cheekiness wanting parenthood forcefully, wanting autonomy but didn't change your decision... the eyes are open.

To those who had to be mothers before time because of poor quality of eggs, and you then agreed... I commend you.
To those who just wanted the seed so they can be mothers... I have learned something.

To those who are not parents distinctively, but have parentism... carry on... I encourage you.
To those who have miscarriages trying motherhood... do not give up on God.
To those who give up their bodies to carry for their sister's, their cousins, friends and those they have never seen because of their love for motherhood... you are right, you are kind.
To those who say, 'I gave birth to children, and they are nothing like me', it's alright when it is well with Him... decisions are His.
To those without a conscience love of motherhood, transacting other people's children... this day is coming to you.
To those who are not mentally stable, but when your minds come back and you are reminded that you are somebody's mother... stay in hope God is the helper.
To those who had a second of motherhood, a minute, an hour, a day, a week, a month, a year... Then the happiness ended whilst enjoying... find comfort.

In all obstacles that you have gone through, it was meant to be and it is alright because you were the chosen ones.

He has not forsaken you but it is then that you are closer to Him.
This too shall pass…
Keep quiet and know… He is God.
In everything know that you are loved… be strong.

Translated from the Xhosa original – Zukiswa Muriel Adonis's Ubumama – *by Innocentia Mhlambi*

HAWKERS

So swiftly they are gone from the kerb
the wrapped women with their trestles,
trays or towels displaying wares
answering the hungers of those dark-risen
and long-journeyed
early off the buses, out of taxis.

You see them at six and seven
before the day gets dirty,
bread loaves piled high, basins
filled with hard-boiled eggs, matches,
fruit and sweets a bright border
for single cigarettes, sickly pale.

You pass again at eight and see
the pavement emptied, commerce concluded.

JAYNE BAULING

NOT ONE OF US

Can I help you?
offering no help, meaning
let me be rid of you
who don't belong.

Are you looking for someone?
because you must
have strayed in here
where you don't fit.

Yes?
no, there is no place
for you who don't look
or sound like us.

Eyes glance your way
moving on as you should
from this entrance
which is not for you.

                JAYNE BAULING

SIXTH SENSE ON *THE LINGA LINGA*

In Inhambane estuary, the late afternoon monsoon
wind blows warm. The dhow creaks, slants
in the waves, lateen sail ballooning out to slope
us through the tepid lagoon into the river mouth.

The unassuming helmsman tells how this dhow
belonged to his great-grandfather – his family
have lived off the fish hauled from this craft comfortably
for over 100 years. He marks the horizon, points now

to the fading land arched in a natural S,
the water is translucent, almost white, sand visible
on the ocean floor. At the lift of his arm, I stumble
to the opposite slate-streaked, wooden slats
lean back, he says – *lean with the boat's weight*;
my hair is a reckless mob; face only inches from the foam;
hundreds of tiny silver fish race in a sea womb
beneath me. In impish delight, he tips the boat

and the waves spray, soaking my kikoi,
hands, eyes, feet – my unfettered laughter
elicited by this sage without labour
– a buoy.

MICHÈLE BETTY

CALLING HOME

when I phone
Sundays
she's cheerful
*I knew
it was you*!

when I don't
that shrugged
smile bows
in nightfall

maybe by
next week
it won't
matter
anymore

MARIKE BEYERS

SUNDAY

I am here to hold someone's voice
against the unmapped space
of a childhood floating out of reach

women in blue coats and long necks
unbearable
the thoughts
holding their heads

they bow down
their words always
on the other side
of an open field

praise songs cast into the sky
so blue
the memory of clouds
etch into the night

                    MARIKE BEYERS

WHAT'S IN A WORD?

Bird

inside a bird is
a grasshopper
or a worm
and a seed
and ancestors

all filled with
sun and soil
star dust and stories
dinosaurs
the Lego of life

don't say bird lightly
the entire universe echoes through this single syllable

                              NICOLA BRIGHTON

NIGHT WALK

Night ghosts the streets,
while overhead lamps
reveal and shadow;

another neighbourhood,
hidden and spare,
emerges away

from surrounding windows
that flicker and glare,
where people swim in aquariums.

Trees finger the stars
and strelitzias are
like cranes with crazed hair.

Under buildings and roads,
forgotten hills,
lost watercourses and springs,

but what stops you in your tracks
are invisible birds,
clicking crickets and frogs,

baboons mumbling in the pines
and the faintest swishing
of porcupine quills.

               CHRISTINE COATES

MPA MOSWENG
Setswana

Tshwenyana e boa bontlha
E a bo e ikilela!
Moswa se lelele go disa
Nako e ise e goroge
Matsapa le mororo o a di itse.

Tlhaba kgobe ka mmitlwa
O itse fa khukhu e imetswe ke morwalo,
Morwalo e tswe e le wa yona
Ratla la tlou ga e se mantlwane
Le tlhaedisitse ba le bantsi thuto.

Morwadiaka se tatamatse thamo
Nkutlwe ke mmago!
Nkutlwe ona o tsewa lapeng
Monate o fela ka bosula
'Tshaba se lela sa matlhotlhapelo.

Itharabologele e santse e le teng
O ikgotsofatse ka go bo keteka,
Go bo keteka ntleng le go tlhokomela
Mpho eo o tla e bona ka mmamoso
Mmamoso o le kwa bogadi.

Go tuntuletsa ga e se morabaraba
O santse o le wa makgabenyana
Se letlelele tshimanyana go go tanya
Watswa ntho e e tlhokileng kalafi
Bokamoso jwa senyegela go ela ruri.

SANNAH CUJANE

TEENAGE PREGNANCY

You know your own weaknesses
Take care and never expose yourself!
Young person, don't rush to parent
Before your time had come
You don't know effort and perseverance

Relax and take your time
And know a tortoise was weighed down
By its own load
Adult games are not a child's play
It has denied a lot of education

Please don't pretend to have grown, my child
Listen I'm your mother
This advice is given at home
Excitement often ends with sadness
The nation decries a tragedy

Rejoice while you still have it
Enjoy celebrating it
To celebrate without caution
You will still have that gift tomorrow
At your in-laws home

A lullaby is not child's play
You are still young
Don't allow small boys to entrap you
And be hurt beyond treatment
And ruin your future forever

Translated from the Setswana original – Sannah Cujane's Mpa Mosweng – *by Goodenough Mashego*

REVOLUTION

even in plain sight
this man begs to exist, to be seen
his hands are bunched together
and surrendered to the air

his hands fish into this sea of people
for whatever might lift him
out of this hole of hunger
he has found himself dug deeper
and deeper into

but he will be avoided
until he can no longer afford to be
until he moves to haul what we call our own
until our cries prove his own existence
until his stomach becomes a thing
that forgets how to listen
as soon as it has spoken

LUTHANDO DLAMINI

THE TONER ON THE PRINTER HAS RUN OUT

The toner on the printer has run out
and the photocopying machine is broken.
The motor on the gate is not working
and the intercom is silent.
The remote for the TV needs a new battery
and the ariel is off its hinges.
The light on the back security beam
is flashing.
The ants have got in again.
The landline has gone dead and there is no ADSL.
The ATM has sucked in the cheque card
and the credit card has expired.
The lights have just gone off.
Load shedding again.
The milk has separated.
The ghost has given up.
The cord on the kettle has frayed.
The cell phone is missing presumed dead, lost or
had a nervous breakdown.
The bedside alarm did not go off this morning.
Late for work,
I get into my bakkie
and turn the key
to start.
Clunk!

CHRIS ELLIS

DIT LYK ALWEE NA REËN
Afrikaans

sê my ma soos sy
by die venster sit
en die wêreld dophou.
die verleë in haar oë is duidelik
en die stres in haar hande wys ook
soos sy op die uitgewaste stoel sit
wat my broer gebring het van 'n uncle wat hy ken.
Alles is hand-me-downs.
Ek staan in die klein donker kombuis
en kyk
by die venster uit.
Die boom op die stoep
block die son maar ek dink sy is reg,
Dit lyk alwee na reën.

KIMBERLY FLANAGAN

LOOKS LIKE RAIN AGAIN

my mom says while
sitting at the window
and watching the world.
The shame in her eyes is clear
the stress in her hands also shows
as she sits on the washed-out chair
my brother brought from an uncle he knows.
Everything is hand-me-downs.
I stand in the small dark kitchen
gazing
out the window.
The tree on the stoep
blocks the sun but I think she's right,
looks like rain again.

Translated from the Afrikaans original – Kimberley
Flanagan's Dit Lyk Alwee Na Reën – *by Pieter Odendaal*

IKHUTSE LEPANTSOLA
Setswana

Direpudi tsa lelapa tsa tsikinyega
Dipilara tsa kgothakgotha
Mmimo wa didimala
Fa dipego di begwa
Tatodi e re o robetse
Go robetse kakapa ya motswako
Jabba kakapa ya go tswakantsha Setswana le Sejatlhapi

Seyalemoya sa botsa Dipotso
Dipotso di feta dikarabo
Fela diphiri le matshwenyego do itsiwe ke mmopi
Naledi ya rona e ile boya batho

Matshidiso nageng ya etsho
Matshidiso fatsheng la etsho

Re lebogela kabelano yam pho ya gago
Setshaba se go tlotlile
Mafaratlhatlha a apere ditshwantsho tsa gago
Go ketekwa sekgantshwane
Ba re Jabba ke kgosi ya motswako

Setswana sa tuma
Wa se kgabisa ka tatso e ntshwa
Mmino o tswakantswe le poko

Le fa re galetse go go bona
Mo seraleng o kgwa ka tlhaa
Re tla ikgomotsa ka mmino
Matsetseleko, matshetshe, puo,

Tiragatso, botlhami mminong wa gago
Fela o dirile monna wa etsho

Ka bokgabane o re file tatso e ntswa ya Hip-Hop
O re iteile ka morumo, morimo le morethetho
Tlhamo tse di tlhwatlhwa.

Tsamaya sentle senatla
Tshedisegang Aforika Borwa
Tshegetsenang badiragatsi
Ya gagwe tema e weditswe.

TSHEPO GAERUPE

REST PANTSULA

The thresholds of the family trembled
Pillars shook
Music went silent
When we heard the news
Tatodi says you have rested
The king of motswako has died
Jabba the icon who mixed Setswana and English

Radio station asked questions
More questions than answers
Secrets and sufferings are known by the Creator
Our star has fallen

Condolensces in our country
Condolensces in our land

We thank you for sharing your gift
The nation praised you
Yours is a picture of confusion
In celebration of an idol
They say Jabba is the king of motswako

Setswana gained prominence
Decorated it with new flavours
Music mixed with praise

Though we miss you
On stage you spit from the cheek
We will console ourselves with music
Meticulousness, proficiency, language

Performance, composition in your music
You did well, countryman

With skill you gave us a new flavour of Hip-Hop
You hit us with morumo morimo and rhythm
Outstanding compositions

Go well gentle giant
Find comfort South Africa
Performers support each other
As for his role, he played it well

Translated from the Setswana original – Tshepo Gaerupe's
Ikhutse Lepantsola – *by Goodenough Mashego*

AGAIN

We didn't ask for this: Life
with its horror and sorrow crowding down, this
pushing away keep on pushing keep making space
for some lightness, some delight.
I dream the dream-leap night-flight
over the eraser fence of understanding, then find
on waking, I'm standing wrong-footed, useless
at meaning. Sliced by the fact-knife,
packaged, deep-frozen, chunks, wading
relentless. How to imagine a way
out, to find ways, living
with this chain that holds us
down to hopeless
cement. Like dogs, keeping watch
over the empty promise of the food bowl, running
tight rings, hurt-footed, caught again, flight
curbed by the taut length of the radial chain. Howling
at the despair-stubborn fence-limit,
fighting the leash of the brain.

DAWN GARISCH

OLD BLOOD

It will not heal:
the old blood is still on the string

I tried to hold the wound in my body
infection eats me, its heat clawing at my body at night

I don't want to cut the string, relinquish these beads,
I try salt water, Dettol, Betadine, impepho smoke and
prayer

Nothing works. Because, my sister tells me,
the old blood is still on the string.

* * *

I collect the eight white beads carefully, as I cut the string.
Not one falls.
I pull the string out, wincing at fresh pain.

it has old and new blood on it.
the string, the old blood

this land

the earth wants something in exchange
for the old blood
to heal this persistent infection

SARAH GODSELL

THE POLITICS OF A WALL

A calling spurfowl
kicks the fresh dust into air
that shines of the dawn

A bushbuck cracks shade
on a dry blanket of brown
that had once been still

Mopane trees sit
as the copper clouds cluster
on glittering veld

The River is sky
edged green in leaves with the birds
drifting on its clouds

The elephant-rock
sits on the sands of wild space
shifting, yet so still

Tall grass sways below
a breeze of patterned heat held
on the giraffe neck

The River Fig Tree
flies in the sound of bulbuls:
loud in the fast light

The track is yellow
and curved sharp like the hornbill,
as is the sunrise

Dark clouds fill the air
of heavy scents and wet fur,
wild in watered dust

The bright sun bird clicks
and the sky glints red and black
upon the tree tips

A squirrel tail flicks
softly in a tree of screams,
and the birds scatter

We make fake fences
protecting the wildest hearts
from all that is tame

                VERNON R.L. HEAD

TIKO RA LOVA
Xitsonga

Leswi se swi tlula mpimo,
Tiko ri hundzuke tlangelani.
Un'wana na un'wana loyi a lavaka ku nghena o nghena.
A ka ha yimeriwi vunyama, ko fohliwa dyambu xi lo hosi.
Vo tala va tisa vubihi, va bazela hi vukungudwana!
Na maphepha ya nawu va hava.
Kambe a va tiendli.
I jarimani yi va patisaka makaya va ha ku rhandza
Loko xivambalana xi bubu va ta endla yini?
Handle ko chavela Afrika-Dzonga?

Tiko ri ta lova
Mali yi hundzukile xindodzi yi hlalela Afrika-Dzonga.
Yi bazela hi ku bebula vukungudwana!
Hi yona yi vohlisaka makhamba ni vadlayi.
A ni yi ba mati tingwenya tietlela!
Van'wana va fundzisiwa yona leswaku va nga vuli nchumu,
Kasi van'wana vo fumbhalerisiwa lomu tibondareni,
Ku endlela leswaku va pfula tiheke ti ku nhwaaa!
Va kota ku nghenetela hi ku rhandza!

Tiko ra lova,
Xuma xi hi tswalele tinxangu to hambanahambana.
Namuntlha hi twa hi ta ndyangu wa ka 'Gupta'
hikokwalaho xona.
Vo 'BOSASA' a ndza ha vuli!
Va dya va sula milomu hikokwalaho ka mali.
Vanghena na laha va nga fanelangiki hi mhaka yona!

A hi pfukeni matandzeni maAfrika-Dzonga,
Hi wisa ku orha ndzilo wa makhamba.
Hi ku xikepe lexi hi fambaka hi xona xa mbombomela!
Xa mbombomela hi lo xi nhwi!
A hi tshikeni ku va vomafanato.
Hi bokoloka nkarhi wa ha pfumela!
Hi pfuna vatukulu va hina,
Hi ku xindondzi lexi xi nga va tlulela na vona!
Hi nga loveriwi hi tiko hi lo honhoo!!

MIYELANI ANTHONIA HLUNGWANI

OUR COUNTRY IS DYING

This is now overboard, this is now beyond ordinary.
The country has now turned into a playground.
Everyone does as they please.
Sacred things are no longer done at night, but at daytime.
Corruption has gotten people into trouble.
Some of these people do not even have lawful
documentation.

But hey, it is not of their own doings.
It is an offshoot of the Germans' actions that forced them
to leave their beloved place.
What will they do if and when the situation is bad?
Besides caring for South Africa?

Our country will vanish in the midst of our eyes.
Mainly because money has turned into a troublesome
worm that has found its place in the land of South Africa
Money drives corruption!

Money is the reason thieves and killers are happy.
Money makes things happen.
It is used to bribe and silence people.
Some receive it by the country boarders,
Just for them to open wide the boarder gates!
Opening them for foreign nationals to come into the state
as they please!

Our country will vanish in the midst of our eyes. Our
country is dying.
Unto our shores money has birthed different types of trouble.

Today we hear of the Gupta family because there is money involved.
Cases like 'BOSASA' I won't even mention.
They eat and wipe clean their mouths because of money.
They steal and cover their steps because of money.
Access to difficult places is granted if one has money!
Money opens all doors.

Let us stop being comfortable fellow South Africans.
Let us put an end to the fire set by these thieves
The ship we are sailing on is set to sink in the sea!
Not only will the ship sink, it will sink way deep into the sea.
Let us quit being copycats,
and change while we still have time!
Let us help our grandchildren.
Let us help them out before the same problematic worm we face jumps over to them.
Let us protect our country before it slips out of our hands!

Translated from the Xitsonga original – Miyelani Anthonia Hlungwani's Tiko Ra Lova – *by Neo Sehlahla*

SOLOMON TSHEKISHO PLAATJE
Xitsonga

U fambile wa ha ri ndzumulo,
A ha ha langutele swo tala eka wena.
Vo tala hi lahlekeriwile,
A ku lahlekeriwangi ndyangu wa wena ntsena.
Hambi ANC na yona yi lahlekeriwile swinene.
Tiko a ndza ha vuli!
Mutumbuluxi wa vandla leri khomeke mfumo wa tiko ra hina!

Swandla swa wena a wu nga pfumeli swi mila nhova.
A wu khoma laha ku hisaka swi languteka.
U fambile wa ha ri ndzumulo,
Makumetlhatsevu wa malembe a wu nga lo kula.
A wu fanele u hanyile ku kota nhenha Nelson Mandela.
Vukona bya wena byi cincile vutomi bya vo tala.
Namuntlha hi na vatsari, vahundzuluxi na van'watipolitiki,
hikokwalaho ka wena!

I ncini a xi ku dya xana xo pfumala vatshunguri?
Hi lahlekeriwile swinene.
Byongo byo kota byaku bya vutshila a hi vangani va nga na byona!
Hikokwalahokayini u nga hanyanga malembe ya tsandza vahlayi?
Kumbe na hina tindzumulo i nge hi vile na nkateko wo ku vona.
Mitirho ya wena a ku ri leyo saseka no naveta!
Yana emahlweni u etlela hi ku rhula Solomon Tshekisho Plaatje!

A va fanele va ku pfunile
Va tsuvula tinayiti leti a ti tlhavetela mbilu na moya waku.
Leswaku u hanya bya xibondze.
U hanya malembe yo tala!

Tiko a ra ha langutele swo tala eka wena.
Kambe a swi na mhaka!
Mikondzo ya wena a ku ri leyo khutaza no naveta.
Vo tala va ta yi landzelela,
Van'wana va le ku yi landzeleleni hi xiviri.

Yana emahlweni u etlela hi ku rhula nhenha ya tinhenha.
Hi ta tshama hi ku tsundzuka hi masiku Solomon
Tshekisho Plaatje!

        MIYELANI ANTHONIA HLUNGWANI

SOLOMON TSHEKISHO PLAATJE

You left us while we were still infants.

We expected many thing from you.
Many of us have suffered a great loss,
It is not only your family that is suffering from your passing on.
Even the ANC is left suffering.
I can't even imagine nor mention how great a loss your passing is to the world.
You are the founder of the ruling party in our nation.

You always stretched out your hand to help nurture humanity.
With your hands you touched some of the most dreadful places.
You left us while we were infants
Only 57 years old, you did not live a long life.
You were supposed to live a much longer life like the great Nelson Mandela.
Your existence has changed the lives of the masses.
Today we have writers, influencers and politicians – all this because of you!

What is it that was troubling you? Why did you choose to endure it? Was there no remedy to cure it?
We have suffered a great loss indeed.
A disciplined mindset is not owned by everyone!
Why did you not live for many years, so many that even mathematicians would fail to count them?

Maybe that way we also would have had the opportunity to see you.
Not only were your works lovely, they were appealing to the eyes of the masses.
Continue to rest in peace Solomon Tshekisho Plaatje!

They should have helped you.
They should have removed all the pins that pieced through your heart and soul,
Just so you could live like a tortoise.
For you to be alive for many years!
The world was expecting a lot from you.
But it is okay!
Your actions and ways of life are now an inspiration.
Many will follow in your footsteps.
Some have already started to walk directly into your footsteps.

Continue to rest in peace. You are a warrior amongst warriors.
We shall remember you in every single day, Solomon Tshekisho Plaatje!

Translated from the Xitsonga original – Miyelani Anthonia Hlungwani's Solomon Tshekisho Plaatje – *by Neo Sehlahla*

MUDYONDZISI WA LUNYA
Xitsonga

A ndzi ku vusiwana ndzi ta byi hlula,
A ndzi ku ndzi ta humelela ndziva dokodela,
A ndzi ku ndzi ta nyungubyisa tatana na manana,
A ndzi nga swi tivi leswaku ndzi ta hlundzuka xibye xa mudyondzisi.

A ndzi ehleketa leswaku mudyondzisi i mutswari,
Leswaku mudyondzisi i makomba-ndlela,
Kambe namutlha ndzi mafamba a borile,
Ndzi hundzeke nyama ya mudyondzisi.

Vurongo ndzi byi komba hi rintiho,
Tibuku ti ala ku nghena,
Ndzi karhele mina,
Ndzi ta vula a ndzi dlaya xikan'we.

MASHIMBYE OWNERS HLUVUKANI

A TEACHER WHO IS A WRONGDOER

I thought I would defeat poverty,
I thought I would prosper and become a doctor,
I thought I would better the lives of my parents,
But I never thought I would hate my teacher like this.

I saw a teacher as a parental figure,
Someone to can guide me along the way.
But today I walk on like rotten meat,
I have now turned into my own teacher's piece meat.

I cannot sleep,
I cannot seem to understand the academic content I engage with.
I am tired of living like this!
But then!
If I speak up he will kill me at once!

Translated from the Xitsonga original – Mashimbye Owners Hluvukani's Mudyondzisi Wa Lunya – *by Neo Sehlahla*

RAIN BULL

Here is a man
There is his gun
He is dead
And the starving bull beside him
the sickle moon of its horns is a bow that bends and sings
for rain
And sings for rain
And sings for rain
To a storm
that the sun rubs away
Now the
bullets spiral back into the barrel
the licking dust dogs are
an arrowhead sprung again from his heel
the land is before him
Look!
Someone is carving an ark
He is laughing
There is the shell of an old house, the smokeblack walls
and the firepot
the cypress cut
and the windows shut
Buck skulls smile in the timeworn veld
to the pick swing song of the windpump's arm
and the broken back of the ground grinds silt
there stands the man on the lizard mud of a dry dam skin
he slides back in time he is barbel-shaped
he hears the feather fly that skims the vlei
then folds the soft drumbeat of a far-off storm
into the flood of long ago

he listens to such things
that is what we can say:
he listened for such things he
startles up with the crows
and ghosts back to the house with his cowhide sack of
bones
knocking against places he does not remember, waking the
volk, we watch him
leading the bull
back to the kraal
with hands cold as rain

ALICE INGGS

UBUQAQAWULI BUKA PLAATJE
Xhosa

Avulekile amazulu kwazalwa uSolomo
Kwesimnyama isizwe uzakusishenxisa isenzo soboni
1876 ulithemba, kwesimnyama isizwe uzisa intethelelo
Martha ubabalwe, unethamsanqa
Kuba umzele unyana onobuqaqawuli

Babemlukuhla, bemxulutya
Suka waqokelela wafaka etyesini wokha umqolomba
Ngaphakathi equlunqa iqhinga
Lokuthothisa izinga lokubulaleka komntu omnyama

Ungqondongqondo oyinzalelwane yaseDoornfontein
Ophuma emgqubeni wesizwe sabaTswana
Indoda ekhuliselwe phantsi kwesisekelo sobuKrestu
Yazinza enyanisweni nakwezopolitiko
Itoliki ebitshintsha iilwimi ngobuciko

Umbhali osulungekileyo nogqwesileyo
Ikholwa elizinikeleyo
1932 ndiyakuzonda, ndiyakonyanya, ndiyakucekisa!
Ndiyakutshutshisa, ndiyakuqalekisa, ndinga
ndingakutshabalalisa!

Iindaba zasasazwa ngeempiko zomoya
USol Plaatje usishiyile tshini ngumhlola!
Obakhe ubomi ubuphilile
Eyakhe indima uyidlalile

KuTshekisho umntu wayesiza kuqala
Kweli ilixa sibeka ezethu iziqu kuqala

Lo mba uye untsonkotha, ugqobhoza
Ukroboza, uthyoboza
Uyatshutshisa ufuna ingqwalasela

Iphi la nkathalo nolwathando wayelubhinqele esinqeni?
Buphi oba buntu noba bunye wayebugxininisa esizweni?
Makube zanyamalala zangcwabeka esingeni
Mhlawumbi zisekhona ntonje sibhidwe ngumthyoli
siziphuthaphutha ebumnyameni

Esikhoyo isizwe siyagwegweleza
Kuyinqaba ukuphuma egusheni
Siyazicinezela, siyazifuthanisela
Uloyiko kukubekana ehlazweni

Ulutsha lwaseAfrika lulodwa
Kwesi isibaya lugquba lodwa
Abezopolitiko bayalulahlekisa, bajulelana ngalo
Bayalumfamekisa, baxhwithaxhwithana ngalo

Boyele iingqondo zizele ngamangunda
Baxakekile benza iintsana
Batshonile emiphandeni
Babakuza ngokusesikweni

Uxinizelelo lwengqondo longamele
Abaphantsi basifulathele
Kuba ulonwabo sihlala silukhangele
Isuke intombi ibuye ifumbethe ngaphambili
Umfana abuye netyala endlwini

Mzali wethu uzusitarhuzisele
Koo gxa bakho usicamagushele [Nithobe ukukhanya
nentethelelo
UQamata aveze icebo, athobe inceba
Amanyange ahlangane, anyakame kucace
Kuba eneneni ilizwe leengqwele liyonakala
Maz'anethole

        SIPHELELE KHAPHETSHU

THE GLORY OF PLAATJE

The heavens opened and Solomon was born
In a dark world you will eradicate the act of sin
1876 you are hope, in a dark world you bring forgiveness
Martha you have been blessed, you are lucky
Because you have given birth to a glorious son

They used to deceive him, and beat him
He just gathered and put in the trunk then built a cave
Inside he was planning a trick
To calm the degree of exploitation of the black person

An expert who is a native of Doornfontein
Who comes from the manure of the Tswana nation
A man nurtured under Christian foundations
Who found refuge in truth and politics
An interpreter who wisely used languages interchangeably

A pure and successful writer
A committed believer
I hate you 1932, I hate you, I hate you!
I am prosecuting you, I curse you, I wish I could destroy you!

News was spread by wings of the air
Sol Plaatje has left us, wow it is an abomination
He has lived his life
He has played his role

To Tshekiso a person came first
At this time we are putting ourselves first

This issue is becoming worse deeper, piercing
Breaking, demolishing
Persecuting it needs consideration

Where is that care and love he was wearing around his waist?
Where is that compassion and that unity he was emphasising to the nation?
Maybe they dissappeard and were buried in the grave site
Maybe they still exist; it's just that we have been deceived, we are looking for them in the dark

The current nation has taken the wrong path
It is difficult coming out of the sheep (darkness)
We oppress ourselves, we are suffocating ourselves
The fear is of embarrassing one another

The youth of Africa is alone
In this, this kraal they are fooling around alone
Politicians are misleading it, they are passing it around to one another
They are blinding them, they are fighting over them

They are dim-witted their minds are preoccupied with foolishness
They are confused creating babies
They have fallen and disappeared into deep caves
they are confused officially

Mental depression is prevailing

The ancestors have turned their backs on us
Because we are forever seeking happiness
Girls just come back-packing in front
And boys come home with charges

Our parent, you must plead for us
And make atonement for us to those of your likes
And you all must bring forth light and forgiveness
And God must reveal a plan, he must bring mercy
And the ancestors congress, and get up and show off
Because in all honesty the nation of champions is breaking down
Thank you

Translated from the Xhosa original – Siphelele Khaphetshu's Ubuqaqawuli Buka Plaatje – *by Innocentia Mhlambi*

UNOMKHUBULWANE WAMI
Zulu

usuku nosuku uyomthola ephithizela
engakhulumi, engakhali, engahleki
mhla ithuba laziveza uyombuka emehlweni
ukubone konke ayikho./Inkosazane ayizikhathazi ngokuba
unobuhle
Ushikizela eshashalazini eshesha mihla le
Eyakhe intokozo uyicinga kusuka liphuma lize
liyozolahla/Owakhe umphefumulo nguwo ongunobuhle
uNomkhubulwane uyikho konke kimi
eyami injabulo ilele kulentende yesandla sakhe
umfutho wokubhakuza enhliziyweni yami uvela
ekumamathekeni kwakhe
izithukuthuku nogqozi engivuka nalo imihla ngemihla/
kusuka emajukujukwini nasekucasheni kwemicabango
yakhe
ngingaba yini uma ngingaphileli yena
ubombuka umbukisise, ubobheka amehlo akhe
inhliziyo yakhe kulapho inekwe khona
ngaze nganokwesaba. Ngiyothini mhla wangifulathela/
ngiyomethemba na oyohlangana naye
uyombona kodwa ubuqu bakhe
uyoyibona na inhlanhla anayo ngaye
uyozibona kodwa ukukhetheka anakho ngokuthandwa
uNomkhubulwane wami?

Phela lona nguye ongihlubula ngembethe
Ongilambisa ngidlile, ngizele ngingalali
Lona nguye engimphilelayo.
Phambi kwakhe ngihambaze noma ubusika bungashubisa
umnkantsha/

Angihlukile nezihlahla ezithi ziqothukelwe amaqabunga
Kepha zime zizinze nasezikhukhuleni imbala
uNomkhubulwane ufana nezimpande kimi
ngaphandle kwakhe ngingafa nokufa.
Angithi kusenguye lona ongesula izinyembezi
engazibonanga
Nguye ongifunza, angondle ngisuthe uma ngingenalutho
Kusenguye lona ongenza injinga uqobo
Kusenguye engimphilelayo noma ezami zingehlule
uNomkhubulwane uyisimanga somuntu/ngibuye
ngingakholwa ukuthi impela uyaphila.
uNomkhubulwane wami

ZANDILE KHUMALO

MY NOMKHUBULWANE

each day you will come across her going up and down
she is not talking, not crying nor laughing
but when opportunity presents itself you will look her in the eye
and see everything that she is
The maiden does not concern herself about being a beauty
she busies herself in the yard every day
her happiness, she seeks from when the sun comes out until it sets
her soul is the one which is beauty
Nomkhubulwane is everything to me
my own happiness is rested in the palm of her hand
the hard beats in my heart originates from her smiles
my sweat and energy that I wake up with everyday
originates from the depths and recesses of her ideas
what will I be if I do not live for her
you must look at her properly, you must look at her eyes
that is where her heart is hung
I am afraid. What will I say the day she leaves me
will I trust whomever she will come across
will that someone see her essence
will that somone realise their luck having her
will that someone realise how special they are by being loved by my Nomkhubulwane

She is indeed the one who undresses me when I am dressed
Who makes me hungry when I have eaten, feel drowsy but fail to go to sleep
This one is the one for whom I am living

Before her I walk about naked even when the winter cold makes the bone marrow freeze
I am not different from the trees that have their leaves plucked out of them
but which also stand firm even when there are floods
Nomkhubulwane is like roots to me
Without her I will surely die indeed
Isn't she who is wiping away my tears which I have not noticed
She is the one who feeds me, takes care of me when I do not have anything
It is indeed her who makes me a rich person
It is indeed her for whom I am living even when my affairs overwhelm me
Nomkhubulwane is an amazing person indeed
I at times do not believe that she is alive
My Nomkhubulwane

Translated from the Zulu original – Zandile Khumalo's Unomkhubulwane Wami – *by Innocentia Mhlambi*

NDI NGAVHA NDO KHAKHA
Tshivenda

Ndo humbula uri Mandela angavha o rengisa shango
fhedzi o ita zwe a konisa zwone
muńwe na muńwe una ndima yawe
yanga ndi ifhio?

Ndo fanyisa tshikolo sa fhethu huno limiwa vhavheregi
sa phuka dzino shumela muvhuso
nazwino tshitifikeiti tshokhavhisa luvhondoni
ṱhamusi ḽinwe ḽa maḓuvha ndi ḓo dzhena muvhusoni

Ndovha ndi tshi vhudza vhathu uri uVowuta azwi ambi
tshithu
ha bebwa dzangano ḽitswuku
zwino ndo ḓi imisela
na tshifenga tshi khaḓi ntendela

Vhano tenda kha Mudzimu, ndo vhaseyesa
ndi tshi sedza nṱha, ndi sa muvhoni
ndi tshiya kerekeni, ndi sa mupfi
vhari ndi sedze nga ngomu hanga, nda ganama ngazwiseyo
ndabva na miṱodzi

Nda ndi sa humbuli uri muthu anga renga lufo lwawe
makete
dzi G.M.O na zwinwe-vho
mitshelo iyari lwadza
vhutshilo ndi phiḽisi

Fhethu ha mahayani ria hu nyala
ri ḓi nyaga 'makhuwani'

hune ra patekanye hone
na ndala iri ida u vhone

Ndi ngavha ndo khakha
fhedzi ndi zwe nda kho vhona zwone
ngoho azwitakadzi
naa mulandu ndi mini?

    ZAMOKWAKHE KUMBE

I MIGHT HAVE BEEN WRONG

I thought Mandela sold us out
But I guess he did what he was able to do.
Everyone has a role to play
What is my role?

I compare the school to a place where leaders are being cultivated,
Like animals working for the government.
Even today a certificate serves as an item used to only decorate the wall.
Maybe one of these days I will also become a member of the ruling government.

I was used to telling people that voting means nothing
But after the birth of the red party,
I myself am ready to vote because the time is right.

I became a laughing stock to those that believe in Jesus.
They laughed at me when I looked up into the sky without seeing Him,
When I went to church even when I could not hear Him.
They told me to look from within myself if I want to find Him.
I cried and rolled on the floor laughing at these words.

I never thought one could buy his one death by the supermarket,
The fruits and vegetables we eat make us ill.
Hence we live by the pill.

We despise rural places and want to see ourselves in urban spaces.
Modern spaces that allow us to party and do all sorts of things, but still come back to be confronted by high levels of hunger.

I might be wrong,
But this is what I see; this is how I see the world.
Truly speaking it is sad; it is a very sad image.
What is the problem?

Translated from the Tshivenda original – Zamokwakhe Kumbe's Ndi Ngavha Ndo Khakha – *by Neo Sehlahla*

DISPATCH FROM WARD C

I
On Tuesday
you wake
walk the back stairs to find a bird
half dead and thrashing
stunned by its own purpose

You count the split wing
the muffled heart –
smallest of all seeds

II
The corridors are the loudest
an artery of wailing
What nicks the heart
drawn tight across all things?

III
I've known rage
the height of a woman
the cloying scent of relaxer
holds the strongest memory
the sweet scabbing
the hairdresser's instructions:
'Let me know when it starts to burn'

IV
I think often of your world
the quotidian washing
the nightly mewling of the street cat

the sun-blind luck of ordinary days

V
My old roommate had a razor blade
secreted in her bra
What had the years been to her?
She read her Bible nightly
Repeated the words:
'Burn for burn, wound for wound, bruise for bruise'

VI
There are rules
'No hookups'
I dream of scarred fingers
and stonewashed linen
Summering at the window
How mere touch
is abundance in the lack

VII
The doctor asks if I know anything of
'intergenerational trauma'
I think of my great grandmother
thirteen and wed
the chicken coup in red earth
the kneaded dough of girl-limbs
the clutch of a doll in one arm
a baby in the other

VIII
They all want to know
what I'll do when I'm 'out there'
God with me: I'll die, and I'll return
I'll wound, and I'll be wounded
I'll swallow the white throat of fear

                  SARAH LUBALA

ILLING ROAD

the air
wears
the assorted scents
of *umuthi*

battle with fruits
and vegetables
on the pavement

and a tavern
coughs out
drunks
with wet gullets
but dried pockets

isiphithiphithi
buses swallowing up
black men
and women

from various
places
of exploitation

ZAMOKUHLE MADINANA

INKOLO YAKWANTU
Xhosa

Yintoni na inkolo yakwantu?
Ndithetha ngenkolo yommtu ontsundu
Umntu ozalwa kweli la se Afrika
Inkolo yabantu abadala

Le nkolo ndithetha ngayo
Yinkolo yokhokho bethu
Yinkolo yomzi ka Phalo
Apho into zo Ntsikana ziphuma khona
Apho kuphuma khona into ezinkulu Onogqawuza

Ndithi kuwe mntu omnyama
Uyilahlelani na le nkolo
Uyibalekani na le nkolo
Xa ndithi inkolo yakwantu
Ndithetha ngenkolo yamanyange

Kunje nje emzini omnyama
Bayakhala abantu abadala bathi niyilahleleni
Xa nishiya lenkolo nishiya okhokho benu
Niyabalahla nithi maxhalanga batyeni

Amathambo elele ukuthula
Ayazibuza ukuba baphi na abantwana be Afrika!
Kuba kaloku babona, ezinye inkolo ziphuma zingena
Baphi na abantwana beli lizwe
Mzi omnyama buyela kwinkolo yokhokho benu
Buyelani kwi nkolo ka Qamata

AFIKILE MADIYA

THE NATIVE BELIEF

What is native belief?
I'm talking about the belief of the black person
A person born in Africa
Belief of the elders

This belief I am talking about
Is the belief of our ancestors
It is the belief of the house of Phalo
Where the sons of Ntsikana come from
Where the great's *oonoNgqawuza* come from

I say to you black person
Why have you abandoned this belief
Why are you running away from this belief
When I say the belief of the native
I'm talking about the belief of the ancestors

It is like this in this nation
The elders are crying saying why have you abandoned
When you leave this belief you leave behind your ancestors
You are abandoning them disposing them for vultures to have them

The bones resting in peace
They are asking where the children of Africa!
Because they saw other beliefs coming and going
Where are the children of this nation

Black people return to the beliefs of your ancestors
Return to the belief of Qamata

Translated from the Xhosa original – Afikile Madiya's
Inkolo Yakwantu – *by Innocentia Mhlambi*

POPPY WREATH

Braai talk fell to border duty
and how to throw a hand grenade.
The men compared notes,
traded Troepie jokes,
berated those who'd escaped conscription:
spineless cowards,
liberal pretenders.

Look what a bloody mess
this country is now anyway.
What were we fighting for?

A poppy wreath leaned against the altar,
understated and alone,
ready for the Sunday service.
A reminder of The Fallen in *all* wars –to honour the dead
and the visibly damaged.

What of the detonated spirits that
share our homes?

CLARE MANICOM

NITHI NGIYO LE IKULULEKO?
Ndebele

Nithi ngiyo le ikululeko?
Eyalwelwa nguNelson Rholihlahla Mandela,
Iiminyaka ematjhumi amabili nakhomba,
Esihlengehlengeni seRobben Island,
Lapha nisabandlululana ngokobuhlanga,

Nithi ngiyo le ikululeko?
Eyafelwa nguSolomon Kalushi Mahlangu,
Lapha aboSopolotiki basabangisana iinkhundla
ePalamende,
Ipalamende iphenduke kwamgade uhlonywa ngezinti,

Nithi ngiyo le ikululeko?
Eyafelwa bafundi bomzabalazo bangoMnyaka ka1976,
UHector Peterson,
Lapha ilutjha lihlezi ekhaya neziqu,
Lingatholi amathuba womsebenzi,

Nithi ngiyo le ikululeko?
Eyalwelwa ngumma uWinnie Madikizela Mandela,
Lapha abomma nabentwana basahlunguphazwa kangaka,
Awa, awa ngiyala,
Akusiyo ikululeko le yeSewula Afrika etja le!

AYANDA MASANGO

ARE YOU SAYING THIS IS THE FREEDOM?

Are you saying this is the freedom?
The one that Nelson Rolihlahla Mandela fought for
For the full twenty-seven years,
In Robben Island,
Where you are discriminating against colour
Are you saying this is the freedom?
That Solomon Kalushi Mahlangu fought died for,
When the politicians are still fighting for positions in parliament,
The parliament has turned into a laughing stock.

Are you saying this is the freedom?
That students died for in the 1976 uprisings,
That Hector Peterson died for?
When the youth is sitting at home with their qualifications,
When there are no job opportunities.

Are you saying this is the freedom?
That Winnie Madikizela-Mandela fought for?
When women and children are still abused,
No, No, No, I deny
This is not the freedom of the new South Africa!

Translated from the Ndebele original – Ayanda Masango's Nithi Ngiyo Le Ikululeko? – *by Sponono Mahlangu*

NIZOKULISA NINI?
Ndebele

Nidlheganelani ningacimi ngamanzi?
Bujadajada bani obunyenyisakobu?
Sithongwana sani enikiswesi?
Ngasuthi niyalibala bonyana emihlanu
Ililize lakolieli...
Izandla zenu zikhikhibele okumbi khulu.
Khese nilise izenzo zenwezi, lisani.

Maye, anithokozi nina!
Nibawe itorho lokusirhelebha,
Saninikela, sanipha amandla ekungewethu.
Ninjenje nithorha ngebanga lethu.
Sajama imijeje amalwelwe bekanyuka,
Sijamela ukukhetha nina,
Sijamela ukulungiselela ingomuso.
Gadesi niphadlhe iinthembiso,
Nikwenzeleni lokho?

Nakubukhahlakhahla nibuwolela ngemigodla,
Amatorho niwanikela beembongo fanana,
Bengubo bona bathoma ngokwendlalela,
Oveza indaba uhlala azitjhejile,
Ngombana uzakupitlizwa lula
Senga yipukani yodede.
Kanti savumelana ngaliphi?

Bugulukudu bani lobu?
Nakumalimenu atjhelela saboya bekonyana,
Mhlamunye nisaphandliwe,
Mhlamunye nisaqaquluka.

Nange kunjalo, qaqulukani nilungise:
Akulile iinsimbi isitjhaba sihlwengiswe.
Silime, sakhe besifunde.
Kube libisi neluju.
Sithulelwe iingwani ziintjhaba zoke.

Gadesi sibhodwe mtlhago nobukirikitjani,
Nabadala bayanghonghoyila, balila ezimathosi
Ngebanga leendakamizwa ezirhubutjhekisa ilutjha,
Nangamapholisa abondela abaphehli beendakamizwa.
Izindlu zesibethamthetho ziphenduke amatatawu,
Ziphenduke amalawu wamahlaya nobudlhayela,
Ngebanga lekohlakalo
Nokungahloniphi isitjhaba kwenu.
Nizokulisa nini?

BONGANI MASILELA

WHEN ARE YOU GOING TO STOP?

Why are you exchanging and not pouring water?
What is this nonsensical up and down all about?
Why are you fast asleep?
It is as if you are busy complaining that five is nothing…
Your hands are full of dirt
Please leave what you are doing, stop it.

You are never thankful!
You have asked a job to help us
We gave it to you, we even gave you our powers.
You are where you are because of us.
We stood long queues and our blood pressures were up.
Waiting to choose you,
Waiting to prepare for the future.
Today you have broken that trust,
Why are you doing that?

You take all the wealth of our country,
You give jobs to your relatives and your children,
Women get jobs by being raped,
The ones who report is always alert,
As he or she can be killed in day light,
He'll die like a fly,
What did we agreed upon?

What greed is this all about?
You are so soft-spoken while you say let sleeping dogs lie,
Maybe you are still in the dark
Maybe you are waking up.
If it is like that you better wake up and fix:

People must be arrested, the nation must be cleaned.
We must plough, build and be educated.
Everything be well and live better
So that the nations can applaud us.

Today, we are surrounded by poverty and corruption,
Even the elders are complaining, they are forever crying
Because of the drugs that kill our youth,
And also about the police who are the transporters of drugs
The legislators has turned into the playing grounds,
They have turned into the grounds where foolish things are pursued,
Solely because of corruption,
And also because of not respecting the nation,
When are you going to stop?

Translated from the Ndebele original – Bongani Masilela's Nizokulisa Nini? – *by Bongani Masilela*

DIVINERS

Prologue

I wonder how shallow this bed is
Its four corners balanced by eight serpents
Their protruding tongues tied and acting like quilts
Tilting my pillows, tightening my feet.
Sometimes I call it *segateledi* – sleep paralysis
(A metaphor for captivity)

They are monsters beneath my bed
A poisoned anthem taught to kids
That are wet behind their ears.
To veil their precious eyes from seeing where healing resides.
I've been slumbering beneath nature's veins.
I clutch for oxygen and consume carbon dioxide
In the process.
But I try to make sweet every bitter
Situation I encounter.
Fuck making lemonades from lemons
I took mangoes and decided to make atchaar.
In my culture
When a child is born
Bird faeces are plastered on top of her head
To prevent the evil bird from eating her brain
(A metaphor for enlightenment)

Our third eyes are polished by residues of a phoenix
Children that have learned how to sleep
On graveyards because of sickness

We pray with cupped hands
Eulogies unfolding between the fingers
Some say we have a touch of death
We can show you the fruit that rots
Before it is unplucked
Stillborns that die before the parents have sex
The ones that drink the antidote before the poisoned chalice chaffs our lips
We can you teach you how to dream
Because we are raised by our aunts.

He sets a table in the presence of maMlambo, my aunt
Whilst we play snakes and ladders
She is a healer by calling
Graduated from beneath the ground,
Springs nestled within her bosoms
Her certificates are water-marked by purity.
I've seen her still turbulent tides
With her eyes.
(A metaphor for silence)

Umancane skins us with her bare hands to prove that she can heal
That she can suck antidotes from mortals
That she can take death and create life
That she cut our faces with razor blades
To protect us from evil
That we sometimes bleed holy purges
Our blood rolled crudely as she makes pilgrimages to divinity.

That we are the river of Gxarha
And she keeps throwing dead cattles at us
Hoping to awaken the new people.
But maMlambo had cancer

Epilogue

I gave her my bed
The eight serpents will carry the tumour beneath their bellies.
The disease has eaten her brain
She tries to work but her thoughts have been liquidated by illusions and hallucinations
The wages of psychosis are social death.
Existence is hemmed between reality and illusion.
I asked mother if we could use bird faeces on my aunt's head
So that she can regain her consciousness.
But Mother said, 'Those who suck antidotes are immune to healing. They become angels with poisoned wings flying aimlessly towards the oblivion.'
My *umancane* passed on.
Her obituary read, 'She came. She healed. And then she passed on.'

LINDA MASILELA

HO SENYEHILE KAE?
Sesotho

Bana ba thari e ntsho
Bana ba Thesele, tjhaba sa Moshoeshoe, Mapara kobo a matle,
Ho senyehile kae?

Dibeng tsa thuto ho dubehile
Madi a tsholoha ntle le tshabo,
Madi a bana ba batho ho phalla
Jo! Ho senyehile kae?

Ntle le qenehelo a bo titjhere a nkwa,
Mong a bo nka ntle le qenehelo,
Wa batho ngwana a shwa fu le sehloho,
Ho senyehile kae, maapara kobo?

Dialemoya, ditheleveshene tsa tsanyaola,
Marangrang a lla nyene, bosiu,
Hohle ha utlwahala seboko,
Boko se bohloko, se hlabang pelo.

Bana kajeno, ke dira ho matitjere,
Ba iphetotse mmutla wa dintjeng,
Ba tsoma ona a matitjhere maphelo,
Jo, ho senychile kae!

Ba nena thuto, ba nyatsa tlhalefo,
Ba bona bokamoso ba bo metsa,
Ba bo akgela tleneng tsa tau, nyaope,
Ho senyehile kae?

Melomong ba tshwela tello,
Pelo tsona di thata sa jwe la moralla
Tsa bona diatla di kgenathetse madi,
Madi a bana ba batho a botswa ho bona.

Ruri la mmuso letsoho le maruru,
Le tletse mosa, le tletse qenehelo,
Kajeno kotlo ntjheme o fuwa e bobebe,
Ba hae phelo bo a nolofatswa.

Wa batho ngwana lena o le furaletse
E se ya hae thato a le furalla
Hohle ha utlwahala dillo, ditsikitlano,
Ruri lena fatshe le soto, kgopo.

A thekenoloji marangrang a phatlalatsa
A phatlalatsa tse bohloko ditaba,
Tsona tsa ho nyahamisa mmoko
Ho senyehile kae, Maapara kobo?

Diqhoku tsa thuto, marobatjhoko ra sekama,
Ra seka meokgo, ra taboha dipelo,
Wa rona mmuso o re ila sekgethe,
Jo, ho senyehile kae?

Tsa bana dikolo di nkelwa hodimo,
Matlamathae kajeno ke dintja, mehofe,
Ba tellwa le ke leseaqheme, tsipasehole
Ho senyehile kae, Afrika Borwa?

A rona maphelo bana ba metsa,
A fela jwaloka a dintsintsi, di tlepetswa,
Hohle mapatlelong ha utlwaha diboko,
Boko sa ho se hlomole ntjheme pelo.

Ruri Afrika Borwa e dubehile!
Hlabang mokgosi le qahamise ditsebe,
Lwanang ena ntwa, ka boqhetseke,
Emang ka maoto le e late letaiyane.

Ba Afrika Borwa bokamoso bo lerothong,
Ruri fifi lona ke la bokantjana, ho ntjheme,
Howang ka le phefa lentswe, le hlabe mokgosi
Hoba ya ntjheme pelo , e thata sa jwe la moralla.
Tsoho le kgenathetse madi, ditshila, la ntjheme,
Wa hae molomo o tshwela dihaeba, dikakata
Ke bolela yona tjhefu ya masumo sebele,
Jo, ho senyehile kae, baithuti?

Hlabang mokgosi, maroba tjhoko,
Ya lefu tsenene e hlabile, e phuntse,
Ya ratha, ya ranthanya dibeng tsa thuto,
Ya sia mathata, masisa-pelo, tsona ditlokotsi.

Wele! Tjhaba sa Ramasedi, Mmopi,
Wang ka magole le etse thapedi, matlama-thae
E tswe moleko o hlolwa ka thapelo, mokanaka,
Ho senyehile kae, badumedi, barapedi?

Phahamelang mapoqo le sa tjhabile,
Wena yunione lwanela ba hao basebetsi,
Tsa bona tokelo o di lwanele, o di tseke,
Fina seledu o lwane ya dibono ntwa.

Bana ba batho ba fela o le teng,
Ba qetwa ke ngwana, leseaqheme,
Ru le letsohadi la aparela la thuto lefapha
Afrika Borwa, ho senyehile kae?

Ipopong kgonyanyana phiri, ngatana-nngwe
Batswadi, Mmuso, Yunione lona baithuti,
Ena ntwa re e lwane sedutse, re e fenye,
Etswe tshwele le beta poho, mmoho re ka kgona.

Sa a rona matitjhere riti se kgutle,
Ba rona bana ba hlomphe, ba boulele,
Etswe e kojwa esale metsi thupa,
Ke wa ka mangole, ke phahamisa diatla
Ho etsa thapedi, wele tjhaba sa Rantsho!

AARON MPHO MASOWA

WHERE DID WE GO WRONG?

Black nation
Children of Thesele, Nation of Moshoeshoe
Beautiful children of the soil
Where did we go wrong?

There is chaos in educational institutions
Without fear blood is being spilled
Children's blood flows
Oh! Where did we go wrong?

Without pity they took the lives
They took it without pity
The poor child died a painful death
Where did we go wrong, children of the soil?

Radios and televisions burst into song
Networks buzz, at night
There's crying everywhere
Heart-wrenching cries that pierce the heart

Children today are enemies of teachers
They have turned themselves into victims
They hunt the lives of teachers
Oh my God, where did we go wrong?

They avoid education, detest wisdom
They swallow their own future
They throw it into a lion's jaw – nyaope
Where did we go wrong?

Out of their mouths comes disrespect
Their hearts are hard like an igneous rock
Their hands are dripping in blood
The blood they shed is visited upon them

Indeed the hand of government is cold
It's full of kindness, it's full of pity
Today a fool gets a light punishment
Life at home is simplified

Poor child is no more
Not his will but he died anyway
Cries and gnashing of teeth is everywhere
Indeed this world is cruel

Networks of technology spread
They spread painful news
That depresses a person's mind
Where have we gone wrong, fellow citizens?

Heroes of education, we teachers lean
We shed tears, our hearts are torn
Our government has abandoned us
Oh, where did we go wrong?

Children schools are taken seriously
Teachers are today's dogs, vagrants
They are taunted even by a flatterer, halfwit
Where did we go wrong, South Africa?

Our lives children just swallow
They are wiped like flies, stoned
You hear cries everywhere
A cry that does not tear a fool's heart

South Africa is topsy-turvy
Call for help and raise your ears
Fight this war, with devout passion
Stand on your feet and confront it

South Africa's future is dim
This is deep darkness to a fool,
Raise your voice and call for help
Because the heart of a fool is hard like igneous rock
A fool's hand drips blood and dirt
His mouth spits vulgar tribulations
I'm talking about a cobra's venom
Oh, where have learners gone wrong?

Call for help, teachers
Death's spear has stabbed, it has pierced
It struck, tore through educational institutions
It left disaster, heart-wrenching emergencies

Our Father, Nation of the Creator
Kneel down and pray, teachers
Prayers defeat temptation, my brother
What has gone wrong, the faithful and worshippers?

Stand up and rush while the sun shines
Unions must fight for the workers
Fight for their rights, uphold them

Chin up and fight to the bitter end

Children die under your care
They are killed by a child, a flatterer
A dark cloud hangs over the department of education
Where have we gone wrong, South Africa?

Unity is strength
Parents, government, unions and learners
Let's fight this war together and triumph
There's unity in numbers, together we can

Let us restore the dignity of our teachers
Our children respect and be jealous
Clay is moulded while still wet
I fall on my knees and raise my hands
As in prayer, let it be Black Natio!

Translated from the Sesotho original – Masowa Aaron
Mpho's Ho Senyehile Kae? – *by Goodenough Mashego*

FOR THE BROKEN BOY

Lord, heal the dismembered,
the broken-hearted
and the disillusioned

Lord, heal the broken boy,
who died in 1955,
and many others like him,
who were buried in the dark

Bring back the broken boy, Lord
sew him up
whole again,
the broken wrists, Lord
put them right again
take the slit off ear,
stitch it on again
take the gauged-out eye,
put it back in place
take the grated cheeks,
run your hands along the tears
take the welled-up face,
take the cut-out tongue,
take the broken bones,
put him together again,
Amen.

TEBOGO MATSHANA

SASIPHI NA ISAZELA?
Xhosa

'Ndifun' afe, lenj' inguyis' izobhadla.'
'Utshil' efung' efelwe sisazel' ezimisel' ukumlahla.
Rhwatsha-rhwatsha, walirhol' irhonya lengxow' emdaka.
Ngw' a! Ngw' a! Yagxwala yancam' imvek' ibhonga.
Wamsongela ngesaka wacimela wamphosa, 'walakahla!'

Yasala kuloo mgqomo loo mfambilin' inkolo-nkoloza.
Yaqhaqhazel' inqinqiz' amaziny' indlal' izihlafunela.
Sasiphi na isazela kunina mhl' emlahla?
'Awu! Yaaya phi n' imfobe ebantwini nenimba?'
'Wakhuz' umagez' ezingel' isidlo sakusasa.
Hlasi olo sana walusa kumzi weenkedama.

Bamthiy' ooNontlalo-ntle bathi nguAkhanya.
Wancakathis' ekhul' ekhululekile, wamimitheka.
Bimbilili enomsil' imfund' akukhula wayiqongqotha.
Namhlanje nguNontlalo-ntl' ophum' izandla.
Mandla ngonin' ecel' uSASSA ngeny' intsasa, suk' abazana.

Chiphi-chiph' unin' ebon' isiva, samdl' isazel' emfanisa.
Wamnced' uAkhanya engaz' ukub' unced' unina.
Namhlanje nguy' owonga ondle unina.
Ukuza kwakhe kulo mhlaba yindaba yakwamkhoz' akakaz' amtyel' unina.
Kazi sasiduke phi n' isazela kunina mhl' emlahla?

MZOLI MAVIMBELA

WHERE WAS HIS/HER CONSCIENCE?

'I want him to die, so that this dog of a father can grow up.'
She said with a dead conscience, content and determined to throw him/her away.
(sound of fidgeting reaching for the sack), she pulled out a dirty sack.
(Sound of baby crying)! The baby cried out loud. She wrapped him with the sack, closed her eyes and tossed (sound of baby dropping)

That tiny baby remained in that dustbin crying.
He got cold, his teeth clashing together, hunger eating away at him.
Where was her conscience the day she threw him/her away?
'Ahh! What happened to understanding and love in people?'
The mentally disturbed man shouted in astonishment while looking to find breakfast.
Picked up that baby and took it to the orphanage home.

The social workers named him/her Akhanya.
He gradually grew up free, and smiled.
He went, confidently, into higher education as he grew up.
Today s/he is a very successful social worker.
Meeting his/her mother at SASSA one day, and they did not know each other

Teary, the mother seeing a birthmark, her conscience eating her, when she recognised her/him.

Akhanya helped her not knowing he is helping his mother.
Today it is him taking care of his mother.
Him coming into the world is an issue of the in-laws he
has never been told by her/his mother.
I wonder where the mother's conscience disappeared to
the day she threw him away?

Translated from the Xhosa original – Mzoli Mavimbela's
Sasiphi Na Isazela? – *by Innocentia Mhlambi*

CARNIVORE

Early Sunday morning,
hunters' shots reverb across the valley.
kudu, springbok, hartebeest flee;
tiny in my binoculars.

Across town the abattoir
sits, squat and unremarkable,
overlooking farms:
game/beef/game/beef.

The air carries the scents
of the bush, not
of animal blood and terror,
yet the landscape feels unsafe.

I flinch at every shot.
Defrosting in the kitchen sink,
Three, thick rump steaks
rebuke me.

JEANNIE WALLACE MCKEOWN

DANCE WITH US IN LAVENDER HILL, MY CHILD

Do a dance with daddy
Before I shave and don my boots
Before I head out (leaning into the wind)
To pack and stack the orange and greens
At the fruit and veggie stall

Do a jig with mammie
as she stirs your porridge
Then, later, takes a pot of *vetkoek*
to the gates of learning
that still prevail along our street

Do a jive inside your head
As you ride the swing
At the high point, you'll see Vrygrond
At the lowest, you'll spy the sandy sand
On which we built our house

Dance with us, your ma and dê
Be happy, little girl;
And, *ja*, we do know
There are thorns and petals
In our dusty little world

FRANK MEINTJIES

AUTUMN

Autumn is the season of blood. The birds know,
the weather vanes of their thin bones point out
to the panting night. It's only the small creatures
who are wise, who dig deep enough to shroud their breath

from the trees, throwing off their colours and clawing
the turncoat sky. It's the dizzy orgy of sun and sap
that makes us forget. Makes us make believe we aren't just gifts
that life shoves in the arms of dumb death.

Time will always crawl from the belly of the world –
from the blood of sun-torn leaves.
The agony of flowers will force its black dreaming –
always – from the sloughed, bright carapace of summer.

JANINE MILNE

MOTHER OF KNIVES

From my chipped Formica dreams you still lean,
your fingers peeled like potatoes to their pink quick;

tracing out the alphabet of how to take a skin
and find a man in it. A for Adam, B for Brett, C for Christ how memory

throws me to that same seething grate, the kettle screaming
please sweet Jesus not tonight. Mother of knives

am I still your chosen, your little bullyrag, cloven as the devil's foot?
will the blackmouth stove always sing its songs to daddy

who waits at the table simmering under half-closed lids
while moths tick tick tick the light like undetonated bombs?

I've paid the moon in my own dark runny honey again
and again. Sunday, there is no *after church*, the ice doesn't clink

or oil my lovers fists, yet truth be told I grow my own beast
of him. Day after day I offer my spoonmeat heart in your old white

bowl that's more shard than whole. Like a drug he will learn
to love me served in the goading of my own pink blood.

JANINE MILNE

BOTSANA
Sepedi

Ge o ka goroga ka setu
Direto di le ntshe
Ke tlare go mang
Ntebalele?

Go katetšwe moya teng ga gago,
Ka molomo wa tshwa koša
Molodi wa sello.

Dinao tša difokeng di alelwa mekgopa
Ya swana le khulong tša mošate
Wena wa bonwa o letwa ka thedi
Go hlabja mokgoši.

Rrago ke mmetla-mantšu,
Sešoga-melodi.
Tša gago dipheta
ba tšea malebiša.
Geno bokgabo ke sediba
Botsana bo runya mobung,
Bohlatse re bea wena pele.

Letago la gago
O feteditšwe ke yoo mmago
Ka go nanya le Boiketlo
O swana le bomakgolw'ago

Wena mošalalapeng la Madingwaneng
'Šaka le re agela wena
Kholofelo re thekgile ka wena

MATETE MOTSOALEDI

BEAUTY

If you arrived in silence
While praise poems are in abundance
To who shall I say
Forgive me?

You are burning inside
Out of your mouth comes forward a song
A crying whisper

Those from royalty sit on a cow hide
Like a royal herd of cattle
People kneel when they see you
Ululations follow

Your father is a wordsmith
Sculptor of sounds
Your beads
Many emulate
Aesthetics resides at your place
Beauty sprouts from the ground
We put you first as proof

Your glory
Inherited from your mother
To tiptoe and serenity
You took from your grandmother

You custodian of the Madingwaneng heritage
This kraal we erect for you
We put our trust in you

Translated from the Sepedi original – Matete Motsoaledi's
Botsana – *by Goodenough Mashego*

MY MOTHER TONGUE

They say a child acquires a language by spending two years listening to its sounds.
I never followed up to the next stage.
I begged my tongue to click, to pull, to gag
To dig into my throat where my ancestors waited for me to give back.
But it hasn't forgiven since the day I thought English was better.
My begging has only given me sorry conversations of me listening and them speaking.
Speaking in honoring the very ancestors that I neglected to give back.
And now my language is buried in a bag filled with holes.
And I am carrying this bag while losing the very little that I am pitifully trying to salvage.

ZIMKITHA MPATHENI

NGIYIMPUMPUTHE
Zulu

'Mzuzwana kawuvamile ukuhlala isikhathi eside
Sikhathi eside ungaphenduka umzuzu ngomzuzwana nje'

Ngikuthande ngomphefumulo wami nangezitho zami zomzimba
Ngizinikele ngakho konke kuwe ngasala ngingenami kimi

Namhlanje kangizazi ukuba ngingubani
Konke engikholelwa kukho kufuze wena
Amaphupho ami...
Isandla sakho angeke sangidida naseningini ngisho sesashwabaniswa yiminyaka
Imigqa yaso ngiyazi njengesikhathi esingaphansi kwemizuzwana
ehlukanisa ukushaya kwenhliziyo yakho

Ngithe uthando kaluboni
Wangenza ngalibala ukuba ngiyimpumputhe
Sengaba yinto ehamba idwanguza nje buhle bukamoya uswele umzimba
Bethi sasike sasho sathi abafana bayizinja
Pho ke mina ngililelani ngoba bake bangixwayisa ozakwethu
Ngama ngelithi owami ngamlethelwa yizinyanya
Ngithi izinhliziyo zethu zahlanganiswa ngabangaphambili kwethu
thina singekabi nangumcabango
Ngithi uthando lwethu ludala kakhulu kuneminyaka yethu

Engithi phela mina ngiyimpumputhe

Bengibiza ngamagama baze bethi siyoke sibone, nanka ankanke umbombo
Senza njani ke uma wena sowathatha impilo wayibeka lapha namhlanje?
Uma sowaphula izithembiso ezakhiwa nguwe nxashana
Ungicathulisa ngothando uze ufunge nangephakade uqobo
Uke walanda ikusasa walibeka kwinamuhla
 Nami ngazibona ngiyingxenye yakho konke okukhazimulayo
Ngizithanda kanjani ke kodwa namhlanje?
Ngizithemba kanjani ke kodwa namhlanje?
Ngisayikho konke yini lokhu obukade ungibona ngiyikho izolo?
Namhlanje kangizazi ukuba ngingubani
Ngifisa ukulibala konke ngize ngilibale nemicabango engami imbala
Ngicela ukuba yingxenye yokungekho, ngigwinye moya
Sengihamba ngibhadula nje ngihamba
Ngicinga amaqophelo ezinyawo zami eminyaka engamashumi amabili nane adlulayo
Hleze angithathe angibuyisele esibelethweni sikamame
KwaMnyama kuphela akukho okuqhathaniswa nokunye njengakwaMhlaba
Uthando lungancikanga kwizenzo kepha
kwimizwa efika nemilolozelo yezigi zenhliziyo kamame
Mina...
ngiyimpumputhe kanti futhi nginjalo nje
 kangizazi ukuba ngingubani

KWAZI NDLANGISA

I AM BLIND

'Seconds, you are not accustomed to linger for a long time.
Long time, you can turn into a short time within seconds.'

I have loved you with my soul and my parts of the body
I have given all of me to you and I ended up unhappy with myself

Today I do not know who I am
Everything that I believe in takes after you
My dreams…
Your hand will never confuse me among the throngs even when it has been made to wrinkle up in these years
Its lines I know just as I know time, which is under its seconds
that separates the beating of your heart

I said love does not see
You made me to be preoccupied by being a blind person
I have been reduced to walk aimlessly like the beauty of the soul without a body
Adage has once pointed out that boys are dogs
So why should I despair because I have been warned by my peers
I stood by my grounds saying he has been brought to me by my ancestors
I said our hearts were joined by those who came before us long before we were even thought
I say our love is older than our years
Isn't that I am a blind person

They called me names saying, we shall see, here are the
eyes bordering the snout
What shall we do when you take life and carry it on your
back?
When you break promises that you build when
You walked me slowly through love and even swear by
eternity
You even fetched tomorrow and placed it in front of today
I even saw myself as part of everything that glittered
How do I love myself today?
How do I trust myself today?
Am I still everything that you said you saw in me
yesterday?
Today I do not know who I am
I wish to forget everything including forgetting about
myself too
I pray for being part of what does not exist, to be
swallowed by air
Now I walk haphazardly I go about
Looking for the edges of my feet of twenty-two years that
has gone by
Perhaps they will take me back to the womb of my mother
At the place of Darkness where there is nothing to be
compared to that on the place which is Earth
Where love is not dependent on actions but
on the feelings that come with the rhythms of the lullaby
from the heart of mother

I…
am a blind person and furthermore
I do not know who I am

Translated from the Zulu original – Kwazi Ndlangisa's
Ngiyimpumputhe – *by Innocentia Mhlambi*

NGIYINGXENYE YOMOYA
Zulu

Inyanga isigcwale izihlandla zantathu ngivika ukufa
Nginqanda umphefumulo lapho uphatha ukungiphunyuka
Ngingaqali ke nokho nokuzibona nginyamalala,
ngiba yingxenye yomoya
Indodakazi kaMkhulu uNkawu isike yavuka
ngobumnyama iyongibheka emalibeni
Ekhuza ibhadi, ekhala ethi,
kungani engatshelwanga ngokudlula kwami emhlabeni
Umoya umhlebela ukuba sengivakashele kwelamaThongo
Sekungathi ke manje usephambana ngekhanda
Kanti ithongo likhanyisa imfihlakalo
Hleze indodana itshethe ifu elimnyama

Eqinisweni lokhu kufike njengesikhumbuzo sokuba mina,
ngisamelwe ukuba nomhlangano nakho konke okungenza
ngibe yimi
Inkinga ukuxhumanisa imimoya emihle engembethe
nomoya wami
Umoya wami,
nokuxabana komqondo
Imilayezo evela kwizithunywa zikaMenzi ngiyamukela
kanjani
ngisahlulwa ukuzamukela mina kimi
Amaxhegokazi asafika izihlandla zazine eminyakeni
ehlukahlukene,
engitshengisa ukukhanya okusebumnyameni
Ngakhala ngokuba bonke bakhuluma ulimi
lwasemkhathini
Ngalibala ukufunda umuzwa womlayezo kwiphunga
lomoya

Impilo indala kakhulu kunomuntu,
injalo nje ibanzi
Uma ufuna ukuyizwa nxa ikhuluma nawe kufuze ufunde
ukuzilibala ubuwena...
Bonke
Fika empilweni uhambaze
Wafika empilweni uhambaze
Impilo kayizazi izimfundiso zezwe
Kepha yazi isibuko sayo,
ubuze bakho

                        KWAZI NDLANGISA

I AM PART OF THE WIND

The moon had become full three times since I have been ducking away from death
Preventing the soul from slipping away
Though it was not for the first time that I saw myself disappearing,
becoming part of the air
The daughter of Mkhulu Nkawu has once awoken in the dark night to go check me at the grave
Shouting abominations, crying, saying
why wasn't she notified of my passing away from the earth
The air whispering to her telling her that I have since visited the ancestors
Now it seems she is going crazy
Yet, it is the ancestor who is shedding lights on a secret
Perhaps the son is carrying a dark cloud

In actual truth this came upon me like a reminder that I am still awaited to have a meeting with everything that makes me who I am
The problem is connecting all the good spirits that have covered me
with my spirit
My spirit,
and the conflict of my mind
The message from the messengers of the Creator, how do I accept them
when I am still struggling with accepting myself
The female ancestors have since come four times in different years,

showing me the light which is in the darkness
I cried saying all of them spoke the language of outer space

I preoccupied myself by reading the feeling of the message from the smell of the air
Life is older than man
And it is also broad
When you want to hear talk, you must also learn to forget about yourself…
All of you
Come to life with nothing
You came to life with nothing
Life does not know the teaching of the world
But it knows its mirror,
your nothingness

Translated from the Zulu original – Kwazi Ndlangisa's Ngiyingxenye Yomoya – *by Innocentia Mhlambi*

KWANGA
Zulu

Umvelinqangi ezibona okokuqala
Ubuciko obungabonwa ngeso lenyama
Ukuphila kukaMoya
Uthando
Ukuzalwa komhlaba
UNomkhubulwane ezibusa siqu
Umphefumulo wokuqala emhlabeni ukwanga
Uthando ukupheleliswa kwakho konke okunobudlelwane
obuhle nenhliziyo
noMoya ohlanzekileyo

Iphupho liphefumulelwa uthando
Ukukhanya okungenamini nabusuku,
Kuziveze kithi kungekafiki nasemhlabeni,
Come and join us on the 23rd of this month as we will be celebrating all that is LOVE.
On the lineup we have Ceb'sile Shwazile KaMakhedama, Prayzer Imbongi, Siya Lumko Tshazi and Noluthando MlawuzaKungekabi nangumcabango
Uyikho konke okwafika namaphupho, nalapho kudalwa khona umcabango
Omunye ethi, 'uzofana nawe ngamehlo nangomlomo'
Nomunye ethi, 'uzofana nawe ngesiphongo nangekhala'
Bephimisa konke okuhle, bedala iZulu emhlabeni
Bethi,'Kwanga Umvelinqangi nayo yonke imiMoya emihle ingakwanga ngothando,
Ikuvikele emeveni wezwe ukuze uzokhula uvike izwe, ulange ngothando'
Izifiso zabazali zingahambi nazinsimbi namaketango
Phefumula ngokukhululeka, ngowakho wonke umoya

Nawe ungowakho... wonke
Unamandla wokuzizala kabusha njalo uma kudlula umzuzwana

Mlingo ongenazimfihlo buhle beqiniso lokuqala,
Uthando...
Umvelinqangi eluphe umzimba nomphefumulo
Isikhumbuzo sobubanzi nokujula kweNdalo

Sikubungaza njalo uma sivuka inyama isanoMphefumulo
Sikuculela imilolozelo, kuthi lapho umoyizela iLanga likukhothamele
UMvelinqangi ezibuka isibini, eziqu zine
Ukuphila emhlabeni kungasakhile phezu kwesisekelo senzondo nokusaba
Ukuphila naphakade kufezekiswa
UKwanga uthando,
Ukuphila naphakade.

KWAZI NDLANGISA

IT IS AS THOUGH

The creator seeing himself/herself or them for the first time
The art that cannot be seen by the naked eye
The life of the Soul
Love
The birthing of the earth
Nomkhubulwane reigning by herself
The first breath on earth is a kiss
Love is the completion of all that has a beautiful relationship with the heart
and a pure Soul

A dream is breathed into by love
The light that has no day or night
Appear to all of us before it reaches the earth
Before it even becomes a thought
You are everything that comes with dreams, even where a thought is created
One would say, 'her/his eyes and mouth will look like yours'
And the other will reply, 'his/her forehead and nose will be like yours'
Uttering all that is beautiful, creating a Heaven on earth
Saying, 'It is as though the Creator and all the beautiful Souls can kiss you with love
Protect you from the thorns of the world so that you will grow up and protect yourself from the world, and kiss it with love.'
The wishes of the parents should not be accompanying irons and chains

Breathe freely, all the air/breath is yours
You are of yourself too ... all of you
You have the power to give birth to yourself again when a second passes
Magic that has no secrets truthful beauty of the first Love...
The creator has given it to the body and soul
The reminder of the breadth and depth of Nature

We commemorate you every time when we wake up, the body is still with the soul
We sing lullabies, and when you smile the Sun bows to you
The Creator looking at his/her very self or them, four parts
Life on earth no longer built on the foundations of hatred and fear
Living for eternity being manifested
To Kiss love
Living for eternity

Translated from the Zulu original – Kwazi Ndlangisa's Kwanga – *by Innocentia Mhlambi*

IQHIYA
Xhosa

Umfazi wakwaXhosa umbona ngokunxiba amadakhi
athwale iqhiya
Sikhukhukazi eso ngamantshontsho aso sisoloko
sineqhayiya
Sakuyibhijela kulontlokwana okwe nyamakazi endle, kuye
kuthi vumbululu isidima
Eneneni iqhiya kwelabaxhosa idlala eyona yakhe yankulu
indima

Njengabhobhotyana izidlele zirhonorhono, iimpumlo
zigxigxiza,
imilebe ivuzisasa izinkcwe unozala ngaleqhiya ebeye
andosule
Zingceba zebhotile zakumila kwimbonakalo mhlaba xebe
phantsi kwezonywaya
amanxeba awuvele ebebotshwa aqhinwe ngaleqhiya

Manqindi angina ebusweni bam
Kulomilo ibingenasphelo noogxa bam
Ukwaquka nentlonti kobhuti bam
Elothala leenyembezi ondizalayo uye andosule

Ngqatsini yelanga usana lulele kumondlalo
Likhuselwa kwiimpukane
Nto ezo zizithandela ubuncwane
Kuye kunyanzeleke lugqunywe ngaleqhiya

Ziintombi zakwaxhosa zingqutsuza ukusuka emlanjeni
Leqhiya ibayinkatha ngaphantsi kwezo emele
Abafazi boo'tata bethu besuka kutheza iinkuni

Ngaphantsi kwezonyanda yiqhiya khawubenomfanekiso
xabengcekelele
Ebuntsaneni bam I bhayi lam lakungafumaneki iqhiya
bendibelekwa ngayo
Esikweni apho kumyiyizane
Amakhwelo entshiloza okoMlonji, amagwijo akawantu
esitsho
Umfazi wakwaXhosa leqhiya ubumbona ngayo

Zehlo zimbi ezibahlelayo
Zihlobo ebezithembile ezibajikelayo
Xanduva lomzi owonakeleyo abalithwalayo
Mpatho gadalala abayinyamezelayo

Bantwana abangenambulelo ababasebenzelayo
Zintw'apha ezingenasimilo kwabo bazizalayo
Zizalwane ezingekhompilweni abazinakekelayo
[Noxa zakuphila ububi yinto ezibanqwenelelayo
(Maxeshonke leqhiya ibithe ndwanya loomehlo)

Umfazi wakwaXhosa umbona ngokunxiba amadakhi
athwale iqhiya
Sikhukhukazi eso ngamantshontsho aso sisoloko
sineqhayiya
Sakuyibhijela kulontlokwana okwe nyamakazi endle, kuye
kuthi vumbululu isidima
Eneneni iqhiya kwelabaxhosa idlala eyona yakhe yankulu
indima
Ndikhule ndaqingqa ingqondo yaqiqa amangqina
angandingqinela

Amanqindi katata soloko enqinda-nqinda ubuso
bukanozala leqhiya ingandi ngqinela Iingqele zifika
zigqithe, imimoya iqguth'igqithe kodwa oko yabakho
leqhiya zang'igqithe
Nditsho indlala sele igquba, iintshaba zingqungile zange
nakanye elikhaya ilishiye
Ngoba inexanduva lokukhongozela iinyembezi zabo
waxhatshaziweyo
Yonase iingceba zeentliziyo ezaphukileyo
Ithuthuzele abo emphefumlweni bonakeleyo
Ibabeka ethembeni lona elo libaphelelyo

Iqhiya ibinto ebendiyibona umhla nezolo
Ikwangunobangela wokuba ndingakwazi uzilibala izehlo
ezindehleleyo ngezolo
Impatho gadalala yabasethyini ibiyinto ebiyibona imihla
nezolo
Ndithetha ngamakhaya ekuxatyanwa imihla nezolo apho
kunqongophele khona inzolo

Ndakuyijonga ndiye ndisikeke ngakumbi yinimba
Ngoba kudala yabanathi kwelikhaya nangentsuku apho
esasilala sitye amazimba
Umsebenzi wam njengambongi ngowokuba ndibhodle
inyani yodwa ngolusiba
Kuba isikhukhukazi selesisidala ubomi buzixhwithile
ezaso iintsiba

                    ABONGILE NJAMELA

THE DOEK

You can identify a Xhosa women by her *amadakhi* and a doek over her head
Hen with chicks, always with pride
That when she wraps it around her head, like an animal in the wild her dignity jumps out
In all honesty the doek in the Xhosa nation plays the biggest role

Like a baby the cheeks are filthy, the nostrils are oozing, the lips are dripping with saliva,
my mother with this doek would wipe me clean
pieces of a broken bottle when they have formed on the site of ground, under those feet
the scars would just be wrapped with this doek

Fists come into my face
In those endless fights with my peers/friends
Together with mischief from our older brothers
That library of tears that my birth-giver wipes

Scorches of the sun the baby is sleeping in the made bed
Protected from flies
Things that love sweetness
It becomes a need to cover the baby with this doek
Xhosa girls walk with pride from the river
This doek becomes the support structure under those water buckets
Our fathers' wives coming from gathering wood
Under those wood piles is a doek, imagine them focusing
In my infantile stages when my blanket would be nowhere

to be found, they would use the doek to carry me on their back
At a ceremony where it is a gathering
Whistles sounding like a singer, and native songs being sung
You identify a Xhosa woman with this doek

Devastating situations that happen to them
Friends they trusted that turn against them
Responsibility of a broken home that they carry
Ill-treatment that they endure

Children who are ungrateful that they work for
Things with no manners towards those who give birth to them
Relatives with health problems that they take care of
When they get better though they wish them bad
This whole time this doek looked after those eyes

You can identify a Xhosa women by her *amadakhi* and a doek over her head
Hen with chicks, always with pride
That when she wraps it around her head, like an animal in the wild her dignity jumps out
In all honesty the doek in the Xhosa nation plays the biggest role
I have grown and my mind trained witnesses would testify for me
My dad's fists always punching my mother's face this doek would attest for me

Colds come and go, winds blow in passing but since its
existence this doek never passed
Even when poverty is rife, with enemies standing looking
it has never, not even once, left this home
Because it has a responsibility of collecting the tears of the
abused ones
It takes care of pieces of broken hearts
It comforts those with broken spirits
It puts them in hope those for whom hope has been
depleted

The doek was something I was seeing everyday
It is the cause of me not being able to forget yesterday's
unfolding's that happened to me
The ill-treatment of women was something it saw
everyday
I'm talking about homes that fought everyday where peace
is scarce

When I look at it, I feel for it
Because it has always been with us in this home
My work as a poet is to speak the truth only with this pen
Because the hen has aged, life has weathered its feathers

Translated from the Xhosa original – Abongile Njamela's
Iqhiya – *by Innocentia Mhlambi*

CHRISTMAS LUNCH

To hear her tell it
you would've thought
she thought it funny.

I mean she was laughing
as she told the story
and even her rhetoric was light,
deftly comical in how she recounted
the details.

Her tone so well struck
it fit seamlessly
with the music of conversation
already filtering around the table.

And we all continued happily
with Christmas lunch
using our spoons to pick out
the various delicious varieties
we could group seven colours
and white samp in.
Smiling at wide-eyed nieces and nephews, bouncing on laps
their mouths wide open
though they barely had
anything to say or teeth to chew.

I don't think it was lost on anyone there.
We'd all heard her pray before,
Long, long supplicant soliloquys

that made our knees ache
and gibberish muttering nieces and nephews
fall asleep.

For sure, that very same story
would be mentioned later at night
in prayer
how just a couple of days
before Christmas
a whole village had come together
to burn a woman (and the unfortunate relative that had
tried to save her)
in her own home.
A fire fuelled by suspicions
she was a witch.

Peace and forgiveness
would be wished on the souls
of all parties involved.
And with all her family hunched on their knees around
the living room floor, safe at least for another day, tears
would roll down her cheeks before she finally said amen.

ZUKISANI NONGOGO

THE PERCUSSIONIST

Her husband was a percussionist
Her skin cells knew only one chant
A rhythm beat into it religiously
On starlit, scarlet nights where the Gods cease to exist

Her contusions stored all the noted to his infectious anthem
C majors tap-danced on purple tattoos
Treble clefs hung from a wounded skeleton

The hymn dripped from her lips,
At social gatherings
Or on days where her bones creaked lullabies and her sheathe revealed all the crooked notes

Her husband was a percussionist
Still is,
But he seems to have misplaced his favourite drum kit
The soil, is ever so loyal
It doesn't make a sound when you hit

FUMANE NTLHABANE

LETTER TO HIS FATHER

Father…
I know you boast to your friends
Of what a great son you have,
But you know nothing about raising one.

I'm not asking much of you
I'm not asking for you
To quit your beer,
But to be my father.

I'm not asking much of you
I'm not asking for your inheritance
But that you love me.

I'm not asking much of you
I'm not asking for you to dream for me
But to support me

I'm not asking much of you
I'm not asking for your all
But for your validation

I'm not asking much of you
I'm not asking for you to live for me
But to be present in my life

Filled with anger and rage
As I write this letter.
For you have added no value
In my life, but animosity

But I choose to forgive you.

Fatherhood is not about a
Position. For that's all you've been, a position…
It's not the position that makes the father;
it's the father that makes the position.

Sincerely
Your first-born child.

THULANI NTISANA

BAMBATHA
Zulu

I
siyanikhumbula enalwela lendaba yentela

ngisho noyihlo ubelazi loludaba,
kudala iminyaka yahamba
akaphindanga walibeka ekhaya.

ngaphansi komhlaba namagolide esihlabathini
kungenzeka, ukuthi washona khona lapha eGoli

umzimba wakhe siyawubala kwimpi eyodwa,

isaqhubeka yona leyo yaBambatha

II
ngingunyana wababa wami

nami ngiyalazi loludaba lobunzima,
ngisho manje ungiphethe kabi ubaas

kunzima enyuvesi yaseFuleyisitata
njengesifundiswa esimnyama, inxeba laBongani
kusinda ngisho nokuqubula ikhanda,

ungathi ngithola igolide kanti ngifunana namakinati

ilelinxeba laBambatha
elaphikwa nguGandhi

impi eyodwa, isaqhubeka namanje,

ngaze ngayifela lemali.

        SIHLE NTULI

BAMBATHA

I
we remember all of you who fought for this issue of taxes
even your father knew about this issue
years have gone by
he has never set foot back home again
underneath in the earth with gold
it might happen, that he has died here in Johannesburg
his body is counted in the same battle
it still continues, the one (battle) of Bambatha

II
i am the son of my father
i also know about this difficult issue
even as we speak now, I am maltreated by the bass/boss
it is difficult at the University of the Free State
as a black academic, it is the wound of Bongani
it is difficult to even lift up a head,
it is as though I am receiving gold when I am actually
finding peanuts
it is this wound of Bambatha
which Gandhi denied
the same fight continues even now
how I die for money.

Translated from the Zulu original – Sihle Ntuli's Bambatha
– *by Innocentia Mhlambi*

NDWANGU
Zulu

I
sizophela isikhathi salendwangu
saqala kuphela ngesikathi sobusha bayo

indwangu entsha sha,
izoqala ihlale endlini ingakasebenzi

izindwanga ezintsha zonke ziqala ngokoma
zonke ziqala nephunga lakhothini

ungaze uze uvikele ubusha bendwangu
uphatheka kabi uma uyibona isincolile

lokuncola kokuqala buyabuqeda ubusha
lendwangu ngeke iphinde ifane njengakuqala

II
ngokuhamba kwesikathi
isiyaqala isiyaguga lendwangu

imibala yona ayisagqhami njengakuqala.
ayikafani nezinye izindwangu ezindala
kodwa sizofika isikathi sokuguga maduze.

indaba yokuncola yona ayisakuhluphi

sekuyajika, iyona esikhipa ukuncola

iphunga lakhothini kudala lashona

izindwangu zasendlini zizofela emugqomeni

III
izinyembezi zezinhlungu zobuntu zona azisizi
uzigezela ubuso ngamehlo

kunini lezindwangu
kukhalwa, kusulwa.

uzowuzwa umsindo wokudabuka
uziphumela ngemilomo, kalula njengemifula

sithwele kanzima, sekwiyinjwayelo
inkinga, ukoma kwalamanzi emehlweni

IV
umuntu omnyama ewasha ngendishi

isandla siphatha indwangu
umzimba usulwa ngendwangu

esokudla siphatha insipho eluhlaza
esokunxele siphatha indwangu eshaya umzimba

umsebenzi wendwangu.

umziba osuwaguqiswa itoho,
itoho elathela induku emhlane
ukuvika phantsi komthunzi welanga,
emhlane, umjuluko usuhlangene negazi

ukukhama lendwangu.

kwilempilo yokusebenza
bayasho bathi,
umuntu ugugiswa kwendwangu,

egcina esephoswa emugqomeni
kutholwe omunye omusha engakafiki nasemgodini

bese siyaphindela futhi siqale ekuqaleni.

SIHLE NTULI

GARMENT

I
The lifespan of this garment will come to an end
it started coming to an end at the point of its newness

a brand-new garment
will first be kept inside the house before it is used

all new garments start off first by being dry
all start off with the smell of cotton

you might even protect the newness of the garment
you feel bad when you see it dirty

this first sign of dirt finishes off its newness
this garment will never ever be the same as it was before

II
after some time
this garment starts wearing off/getting old

the colours are not as bright as before
though it is has not reached the stage of older garments
but the time for it to get old will come

the issue with it getting dirty is no longer a problem

things are changing, it is the garment that generates dirt
the smell of cotton has long disappeared

garments of the house will eventually end up in the garbage bin

III
human tears of pain and desperation do not help

you only wash the face through eyes
how long these garments

have been used to wipe tears away

you will hear the sound of mourning
coming out of the mouth, with ease like rivers

we are carrying heavy loads, but we have become accustomed to this
the problem, is the drying up of these waters in the eyes

IV
when a black man washes in a washing basin

his hand carries a garment
the body is wiped dry with a garment

his right hand carries a green bar of soap
his left hand carries a garment with which he thrashes the body

the uses of the garment

the body that is used to be bent down by a casual job
a casual job that brought heavy punishment to the back
to duck under the shadow of the sun
on the back, sweat has been mixed with blood

the garment dries this

in this life of working
they say
a person is predisposed to age like a garment

which ends up being thrown away in the garbage bin
and another will be found to replace him before he is
thrown into the grave

and then we start from the beginning again.

Translated from the Zulu original – Sihle Ntuli's Ndwangu
– *by Innocentia Mhlambi*

TAKUTSHEDZA IWE RAMAPHOSA
Tshivenda

Wo rumiwa
Roupfa u tshi imbelela
"Thuma mina"
Zwino,
Ri kho u ruma
Takutshedza
Uye kha dzi tshilikadzi
Dzo lovhelwaho nga vhaṋe vha nndwani
Dzo welwa nga khombo
Uḽa musi wa khombo
Vhanna vhadzo a vha tsheho
Zwifhondo zwi ḓo ṱhogomelwa nga nnyi iwe vhathu?

Takutshedza iwe Muruṅwa
Imela ḽino shango sa Murwa
Rilise vhunga mulisa wa phedza
Ri hafha ri phedza
Iwe u Mulisa
Rilise sa nngu
Ri ṱhogomele sa vhalisa vha sa dzibonyi nngu dzo xela
Sedzai fhaḽa Ramaphosa
Zwikolo zwoswa
Vhathu vhau a si vhatshinyi
Asi vha pondi
Ndi madondo a ḽi no shango a vha swifhadzaho

Ṱanzwa tshika dza ḽi no

Vhathu vhau asi madzinga-ndevhe
Ndi tshika ya ļi no ivha omisaho dziṱhoho
Ro tshinyalelwa
Ra tshinyadzwa
Ro tshinyala
Ri ṱanzwe
Ri tshene sa lutshele
Sedzai fhaḽa iwe mulisa washu
Matshudeni mañwe a phasiswa ngo ḓiṱana kha vhapfumbudzi
Ndi ḽone Afurika Tshipembe ḽe Tiro a fela ḽone heḽi?
Na ndi yone mini yenei?

Sedza na fhaḽa
Ri rengiselwa mulingo vhu nga zwiambaro
Vhuṱali ndi mini arali pfunzo isa ṱhonifhiwi?
Sedzai na ngeo
Mavhari- vhari ro apfa
Phaḽamende ndi nnḓu ya nndwa ano maḓuvha!
Na ani neti ngo shulula malofha?
U dzhena mushumoni zwi ṱoda tshone tshanḓa nguvhoni
U sina muthu arenṱha, mukulo wa tsiwana ḓowelai maḓi!
Nḓala i ḓo u sutula
Vhapfumi vha nona vha tshi gonya
Tsiwana dzi goba goba na nḓala dzi tshitsa

Takutshedza iwe Ramaphosa
Rilamulele
Ri lila zwibadela
Ri lila dzi bada

Ri lilela mvelaphanḓa
Ri lilela tsireledzo zwanḓani zwa mbava
Ri lila u sa omi
Sa tsiwana i si na vhabebi
Zwisimani rinwa tshika
Malwadze a nḓala o farelela
Ilwa na tshivhi tsho angarelaho ḽi no shango
Takukhedza Ramaphosa, takuwa!

Phalaphala yo lila
Ḽa ṱavha ḽi tshi sedzana na ṋayo dzau
Wo fara pfumo
Ḽi tsireledzaho shango ḽashu
Wa sa thanya, pfumo ḽi do ṱhavha ngoma yau
Hu na mavhanda
O ingamela sa goya
Mavemu o nambatela dzi mbondo
Vha sedzana na ṋayo dzau
Takutshedza iwe Ramaphosa, u gade na ṋayo dzau
Kanda wo ṱalifha
Hu na mipfa kha ḽi no shango

                MUSHAYATHONI NWOVHE

STAND UP RAMAPHOSA

You are being sent out.
We choose you because we heard you sing a song that said
'send me'.
And now we are about to send you out.
Quickly go comfort those widows who are faced with
trouble because they lost their soldiers to the war.
Their men are no more.
Who will be there to take care of the poor orphans?

Take a stand like the chosen leader that you are.
Stand up for this nation because you are the chosen one.
Lead and guide us like a shepherd herding his cattle.
We are here standing like your cattle because you are our
shepherd.

Lead us as if we were your sheep.
Care and long for us like a shepherd who never blinks nor
closes his eyes because he is in search of his lost sheep.
Look right over there, Ramaphosa,
Schools are burning,
Your people are not evildoers,
They are not murders,
It is the stains of this world that define your people as
being bad.

Wash and wipe away the dirt on your teeth.
Your people are not deaf,

Hunger is what makes them to be difficult.
We have incurred damages,
We are being destroyed,
In fact, we are damaged!
Wash us thoroughly and make us clean.
Take care of us like you would do with a newborn baby.
Look over there ohhh leader of our nation,
Some of our learners are made to pass their schooling grades with very embarrassing marks.
Is this the South Africa Tiro dreamt and died for?
Is this the day we have been waiting for?

Take another. Look over there!
There is plenty of temptation, so much that it looks like we are being sold clothing items.
What is knowledge if we do not and cannot respect education?
Look right over here!
We have heard too many sayings.
The parliament is a fighting place these days.
Are you never tired of spilling human blood?
For an ordinary individual to get a job, they would need to bribe someone within the system.
If you know not a person of higher status, no one will hear you out ohhh poor child.
Hunger will wipe you out of the surface of the earth.
The rich keep getting fatter by the day.
The poor are dragged down into the mud by rigid poverty levels.

Get up ohh you Ramaphosa.

Save us!
Our cry is from all walks of life;
From the hospitals,
From the roads,
We all cry for progress!
We cry and plead to be protected from the hand of the thief.
Help us for we are forever crying.
Crying like an orphan without parents.
The fountains give us dirty water.
Too many illnesses are caused by poverty.
Fight for us this enemy that has covered the surface of our land.
Get up and take a stand, Ramaphosa!

The trumpet is sounding and this means it is time.
The sound of this trumpet is directed to you.
With this new dawn you have to focus on your own matters.

You hold on your hands a spear that can and should be used to protect our land.
If you fail to be wise, the spear facing you will pierce your drum and there will be no sound.
Right now there is a beat that can be heard all over.
Look on like a wild cat,
Thieves are busy climbing our walls,
They are looking at every step you take.

Ramaphosa stand up and be cautious of every move you make.
Walk with caution,
The surface of this world has too many thorns.

Translated from the Tshivenda original – Mushayathoni Nwovhe's Takutshedza Iwe Ramaphosa *– by Neo Sehlahla*

ZINGCE M-AFRIKA
Xhosa

Zingce m-Afrika ungangcangcazeli
Zingce ngobu- Afrika unganikezeli
Ungacengi ngezicengo kwela kuni
Ungacamngci ngezasemzini ulahl'imvelo
Zingce ucondobe uxel'u nocand'ecand'amathafa!

Kaloku ukuzazi imvelaphi ngundoqo
Ukuzazi intsukaphi yingqondo
Zithande uthethe ngesidima
Uzidle ngolwimi lwakh'uqhayise
Bhal'amabali imihobe neentsomi
Bhal'iingoma nezicengcelezo

Wakufeza fundisa nomthinjana
Umlisela wezwe lethu unxaniwe
Fundisa kaloku ukukokoswa kolwimi
Wenza njalo nje nomfo kaPlaatje
Ndithetha ngoTshekisho ithanda-zwe
Ngokuthanda iilwimi ze-Afrika de wazifunda
Akanela ukuzifunda nje wazifundisa

Yinina ukuba sizinyhashe ngokwethu iilwimi zethu?
Yinina ukuyolelwa ziilwimi zezizwe?
Kaloku ukuduka kolwimi kukuduka kwesizwe
Ukuduka kolwimi kukuphela kohlanga
Makhe sizingce sitshongole ma-Afrika
Sixabise iilwimi zethu okwegolide

Zibe yimbunguzulu neqhayiya
Zibe ligugu nakwabasakhulayo!

ZUKISWA MERCY PAKAMA

TAKE PRIDE IN YOURSELF, AFRICAN

Take pride in yourself, African, and don't tremble
Take pride in being an African and don't give up
Don't beg with gifts in your land
Don't flaunt with foreign things and lose tradition
Take pride and walk like the walker walking in the woods!

Because knowing where you come from is key
Knowing where you are from is mindfulness
Love yourself and speak with dignity
Embrace your language and flaunt it
Write stories, anthems and fiction stories
Write songs and pleading letters

Once you have accomplished this, teach every child
The children of our nation are thirsty
Teach them how to preserve language
Even the son of Plaatje did so
I'm talking about Tshekiso, the lover of the nation
Because of his love African languages he learnt
He did not get enough from just learning them, he taught them

Why are we neglecting our own languages?
Why are we consumed by other languages of other nations?
You should know that the disappearance of language is the disappearance of the nation
The disappearance of language is the end of the race
Let us take pride and be clear, Africans
Let us value our languages like we do gold

So that they reign and are celebrated
So that they are a pride a joy even to those still growing

Translated from the Xhosa original – Zukiswa Mercy Pakama's Zingce M-Afrika – *by Innocentia Mhlambi*

SESWANTŠHO SA GAGO
Sepedi

Seswantšho sa gago sa mafelelo
Se gana go tloga kgopolong yaka
Se ripagantša pelo yaka
Se nyefiša moya waka
Ke ipona molato
Ke hlotšwe ke go šetša yaka thari
Ke hlokile tsebe ya go kwa sello sa gago
Mahlo a go go bona ge o be o tuntela gare ga megokgo
Bohlale bja go go lemoga
Ke hlokile sebaka sa go go lemoša
Lerato leo ke go ratang ka lona
Boikgantšho bjo bo nkaparelang
Ge ke gopola wena
Lethabo leo le bego le tlala pelo yaka ge ke go bona
Ke paletšwe ke go go gokara
Ka go amoša borutho bja lerato la mme
Ka go phumula dikodumela
Ka tantetša dintho tša gago ka mašela
Ka go tshwara ka seatla
Gare ga meboto le mebotwana ya lefase

Seswantšho sa gago sa mafelelo
Se gana go tloga kgopolong yaka
Ke leka go ikgothatsa ka gore
Ba mona ba o jele ka dihlare
Ba lefetše wa bogale nkadingala
A di lahlela fase tša mo sebela
A hlakantšha tša hlakantšhega
Ba ntšeela wena thari yaka

Seswantšho sa gago sa mafelelo
Se gana go tloga kgopolong yaka
Ke leka go gopola ditshego tša gago
Lentšu la gago le le sese nke molotšana wa nonyana
Mahlo nke dinaletšana
Ke leka go itekola, go itekodišiša
Mohlomongwe ke tla lemoga
Gore go senya ke sentše kae
Ke kgone go lokiša
Mohlomongwe ke tla ikwa bokaone
O ntshwarele ge ke paletšwe ke go kwa sello sa gago

Seswantšho sa gago sa mafelelo
Se gana go tloga kgopolong yaka
O ithalathadile ka magare mo matsogong
O rutha gare ga bodiba bja madi
Seswantšho sa gago sa mafelelo
Se gana go tloga kgopolong yaka

KAGISO MOSIMA PHAKANE

YOUR PICTURE

Your final picture
Refuses to fade from my mind
It wrenches my heart
Weighs heavily on my soul
I feel guilty
I failed to take care of my own
To your cries I was deaf
Blinded to see you as in a pool of tears you swam
Wisdom to notice
Time to warn you
The love I have for you
The pride that overcomes me
When I think of you
The happiness that fills my heart when I saw you
I failed to hug you
Nurse you with warmth of a mother's love
To wipe your tears
Bandage your wounds
Hold your hand
Through hills and valleys

Your final picture
Refuses to depart from my mind
I try to console myself and say
Jealous folks cast a spell on you
Hired the most expensive sangoma to do it
Threw his bones and they whispered back
Concocted powerful muti
They took you away from me

Your final picture
Resists departure from my mind
I try to remember your laughter
Your soft voice serenading like the chirping of birds
Glittering starry eyes
I try to introspect, self-search
Perhaps I will notice
What did I do wrong
So I can remedy the situation
It might make me feel better
Please forgive me for failing to hear your cries

Your final picture
Refuses to leave my mind
With razor blades you sliced your wrists
Swam in a pool of blood
Your final picture
Refuses to leave my mind

Translated from the Sepedi original – Kagiso Mosima Phakane's Seswantšho Sa Gago – *by Goodenough Mashego*

THE MARK OF A FREE AND FAIR ELECTION

This black mark on my thumb
I'm not sure what it means
So I ask anyone who is listening
for answers
that sound the same as the last time this mark appeared
with hope
and disappeared
with time

They say that your nails can tell you a lot about the state
of your health
too pale you may be
anemic, which is to say
your blood is lacking
or it could be a sign
that your liver is drowning in its own fatty
excess of blue labels slapped onto white papers
a warning, however late
that the heart is congested
mobbed
clogged
choking on its own self
importance

They say your nails can tell you a lot about the state
of your health
a dirty yellow stain
is a sign
that a fungus has taken root in the dark damp

crooks
seeking mobility through growth
unchecked
they possess the ability to avoid
detection
living as they must
by the principle
of decomposition
decay
left to rot
they may
they will
they can
they do

They say your nails can tell you a lot about the state
of your health
cracked rippled puffy split
I have seen these come and go
These symptoms all too common
But this black mark persists
And resists being seen
As anything but the sign
of a healthy body of self-governance
But if you read beyond the tracts
put the facts under the microscope
prick the puss to perform
a biopsy
you will see the black mark
for the stain that is slowly spreading across this

our most vital organ
in our state
of being
maybe then we will call it
by its true name
biological as it is
pathological as it has become
this melanoma
the only skin
we cannot live or breathe
under

CATHERINE PRITCHARD

DIE KRUIEMAN
Afrikaans

Die klein karoo lê kaal
en die takkies en die gras
kruip maar stadig
hemel toe.

Die kruieman kyk uit sy venster
oor die vlaktes.
Hy sien die pers blommetjies
en die jakkals se spoor.

Deur sy tandelose glimlag
preek hy die waarheid van die veld:
wat hier is, is genoeg.

Binne-in sy plooie bêre hy die
kennis van vyf-en-negentig jaar
en in sy hande dra hy sy kierie
van verstand.

En hy praat:

O, mense wat haat en onheil broei:
as jy die duisternis kos gee,
dan sal dit groei.

WESLEY ROODT

THE HERBALIST

The Klein Karoo lies naked
and the twigs and grass
slowly crawl
heavenward.

The herbalist looks out his window
across the plains.
He sees the purple little flowers
and the jackal's spoor.

Through his toothless smile
he preaches the truth of the veld:
what's here is enough.

Among wrinkles he stores the
knowledge of ninety-five years
and in his hands he carries his kierie
of wisdom.

And he speaks:

O, people who breed hate and disasterif you feed the
darkness
it will only grow faster.

Translated from the Afrikaans original – Wesley Roodt's
Die Kruieman – *by Pieter Odendaal*

O BE O LE KAE?
Sepedi

…o be o le kae tate?

o ile go hlemiša la mme letswele
wa tsena ka wa seloko monga
direthe wa di paleša manga
gobane se go tlabile ka go biloga sediba
mola meetse o sa a holofetše
nna morwedi a' go, wa ntlhokiša le ya lešidi mengato
wa fetša ka go lokologanya dikgato
wa tsoga ka a bo kgwale mafato
le morago wa se gerule

go be go le boima tate
go gola ke ngatetšwa ka mašela a go gagolwa kobong ya tonkana
go gola re gadika dithotse
go gola re lalela ka bogobe bja go batwa ka letswai
mare a gana go feta mogolong
mola geno ba ehlwa ba tšhatšhamiša tša makhušana
ba fapana le dikgato tša leroto
ke be ke kgona go bona, ka ge re lebane ka meboto
le mohla ba hlabile tše tharo dikgomo, ka wona modiro wa badimo
re kwele ka monkgo wa nama o kotama merumong ya nko tša rena
mmago a goelela ka mokgolokwane wa basadi
a tšhankgetše ka methuhlwana ya setšo
a hlakela le matsogo a go tlala maseka, a re hlodia ka lešata
'yo a sa rego šatee, o a loya!'
baagelane ba be ba laleditšwe ka bontšhi

ge e le lešo lapa mahlo la tshedišwa
rena baagelane ba go lebana ka difero
go be go le boima tate
megokgo ya hloka mekgoko
ge ditlogolo di biletšwa ka mafuri
ba botoga ba apešitšwe dipheta melaleng

...*o be o le kae tate?*

ge mmago a nkorola phatla ka lehlotlo
a mpotša ge ke se 'tlogolo sa 'gwe
tate ke be ke se ka iša tshele ka geno
ke be ke ile go ba tsošetša
ka ge mme tsebe a ntomile, gore beno ke madi 'ešo
ke be ke se ka iša tshele tate
ruri ka sefapano sa morena
ke be ke sa tsebe ge ke tla kopana le dipela di huduga
ke sa tsebe ge tau e hlatšitše mafatla
a mpotša ge ke fafatla
le go gapa nkwe ka lehlare
yena mmago wa tlhokofele nkong
yena wa go hlamukela maledu tše nkego monna
yena ba rego ke mmitše makgolo
yoo ba rego nna naye re amogetšane seina le leina
yoo a mpoditšego tsebe go kwa
gore ga ke tlogolo sa 'gwe
lebile mare seatleng a tshwetše
a ikana ka badimo ba nko tša mafamo

...*o be o le kae tate?*

boa borwa ga bo thome ka wena
ba hlwe ba eya ba boa
kganthe o wena o gagilwe ke lefe lewa?
ga e sa le di eme ka lešimela
e tla o re thuše go kgotsa tšeno ditlotlwane
di gana ge sothwane e swara
di thoma go re hlodia
re šita go di laodiša tšeno, ka ge e le dikhupamarama
mmago yoo a rego nna ke ngwana wa moloi
lehono šo o swaregile
ba mmoni bašemanyana ba madila
bošego bja maabane a šetše ka melatša
lona letswele leo o le antšego le le molaleng
ee, ke yena mmago
a bonwego a phatekgile leswielo ka dirope tša mašošo

...o be o le kae tate?

boa gae o tle o hlakodiše mmago
šo o bopa bja' sebatakgomo
šo o phatloga ka legoa
o thokgwa dikgopo ka ditšhilo
ke badudi ba motse
šo o rwešwa leotwana la sefatanaga molaleng
o a gotetšwa; kgabo e lauma magetleng a motšofe
a re go taboga lešo lefata
a šihlamela ka gare ga tankana yeo re nwelago meetse go yona
a lebantšha phapoši ya bolao ntle le go re reriša
a fihla ipotuka ka mašela

ya ba nke leseanyana la dikgwetšana
re feditše ka go swara mahlaa
re maketše wa dithuri moloi
gare mosegare wa sekgalela

etse, ...o be o le kae tate?

MOSES SELETISHA

WHERE WERE YOU?

...daddy, where were you?

after swimming in my mother's dam
into thin air you disappeared
dust you kicked, as you fled
the muddied well shocked you
as you looked forward to drinking its waters
you denied your daughter the comfort of mere napkins
while you stepped away from responsibility
and escaped the scene like a scared bird

you never looked back

it was hard, daddy
to grow up pampered with pieces of cloth torn from a donkey's saddle
to grow up frying nuts
eating pap relished with salt
struggling to swallow those tiny morsels
while at your homestead they prepared succulent dishes
they dined while we starved
i could see, as we lived on a valley opposite yours
even the day they slaughtered three cows to appease the ancestors
we could only smell the sweet aroma of simmering pots
while your mother loudly ululated in the tradition of our women
dressed in colourful traditional attire
hands on her waist annoying us with her shouting,
'whoever does not ululate is a witch!'

neighbours were invited in large numbers
while our family received no invite
us neighbours in close proximity
it was difficult, dad
our tears fell to the ground
when grandchildren were summoned to the backyard
appearing wearing traditional necklaces

...where were you, dad?

when your mother hit me on the forehead
telling me I was not her grandchild
i was not there to start a fight dad
just to pass my greetings
because mama told me your people are my blood
i was not there to start a fight
i swear in the name of the Lord
i didn't know I would be confronted with violence
not knowing I provoked a fight
she said I was hallucinating
and skating on thin ice
your mother
she who bears beard like a man
the one they say I should call grandmother
she who they say is my blood and namesake
the one who told me an earful
that I am neither her grandchild
she spit on her palm and swore
with the white bones of her ancestors

...where were you, dad?

going south does not start with you
they go and return
in which cliff have you tripped and fell?
since you left
come help us silence your family's ghosts
whenever nightfall comes
their shadows loom large
since we know little about your rituals, we can't mute their noises
your mother who calls me a child of witches
has been caught in her own acts
her occultic behaviour witnessed by drunkards
last night they saw her naked
those breasts you suckled exposed for all, your mother's
seen riding a broom stuck between her shrunken thighs

...where were you, dad?

come home and save your mother
here she is making all the wrong noises
here she is yelling in vain
her ribs cracked with heavy stones
by residents of the village
now they are putting a tyre around her neck
they strike a match; it burns on the shoulders of an elder
as she tries to run
she plunges in a dam where we store potable water
runs into the bedroom without permission

she wraps herself in pieces of cloth
like a month-old baby
at the end we are awestruck
surprised at the sight of a witch
it's not afternoon yet

but…where were you, dad?

Translated from the Sepedi original – Moses Seletisha's O Be O Le Kae? – *by Goodenough Mashego*

EMATYOTYOMBENI
Xhosa

Mgama kwidolophu ezinamagama
Mgama kwizikhululo zenqwelo-moya
Mgama kwimizi yogcino-zilo
Mgama kwizindlu zexabiso
Mgama kudederhu lweevenkile
Mgama kumaziko kaRhulumente
Mgama kuko konke okunomtsalane kubatyeleli;

Zizindlu ezakhiwe ngamacangca,
okwedlwana yehagu neyenkukhu
Zizindlu ezakhiwe ngenkuni
okwentlanti zemfuyo nedladla lombona;

Kwezo zindlu zixineneyo izitalato zimxinwa
Kwezo zindlu zixineneyo, abahlali: babizela ivumba
lomntsontso
babizela ivumba lelindle
batsiba-tsibana nezinyoka, eziphantsi
baphepha-phephana nezinyoka, eziphezulu;

Kwezo zindlu zixineneyo abahlali;
balala bengalelanga belumkele imililo,
bafaka iintsimbi kwiminyango neefestile
bekhusela oku kokwabo, kwabo baminwe-mide nakwizona-
mthetho
balibale ukuba ezontsimbi ngumqobo
ngeemeko ezingxamisekileyo xa befuna ukuphuma
bambi baphethe bezingxwelerha namaxhoba omlilo

Ngamaxesha omoya, ziyaphaphatheka ezo zindlu

Ngamaxesha emvula, zidama ngamanzi ezo zindlu
Ngamaxesha obusika, zingumkhenkce ukubanda ezo zindlu
Ngamaxesha ehlobo, zingumlilo bubushushu ezo zindlu;

Kwezo zindlu sinyamezele obo bomi
Kwezo zindlu sinyamezele loo ntlungu!
Kwezo zindlu siphila loo ntlalo!

            SIWAPHIWE FORTUNE SHWENI

AT THE INFORMAL SETTLEMENTS

Distant from cities with big names
Distant from airports
Distant from houses of law
Distant from expensive houses
Distant from a variety of shops
Distant from government departments
Distant from everything that attracts tourists;

Are houses built from rusting metal sheets
Like a pig sty and a chicken coop
Are houses built from sticks
Like a kraal for stock and house for harvested dry corn

In those houses that are over packed and streets over populated
In those houses that are over packed, residents:
breathe in the scent of urine
breathe in the scent of faeces
they jump over live electricity cables, on the ground
they duck live electricity cables above them

In those swamped house, residents;
sleep with one eye open, cautious of fires
put metal bars on their doors and windows
protecting themselves, from thieves and crime offenders
forgetting that these metal bars are an obstacle
during hurried situations when they need to get outside
As a result they are victims of fires

During windy times, those houses are blown away

During rainy times, those houses are flooded
During winter, those houses are freezing cold
In summer, those houses overheat
In those houses we endure that kind of life
In those houses we endure that pain!
In those houses we live that kind of life!

Translated from the Xhosa original – Siwaphiwe Fortune Shweni's Ematyotyombeni – *by Innocentia Mhlambi*

DEPRESSIVE EPISODES

I
I don't feel too good. Getting out of bed in the morning is difficult
and it's been a long time since I've had a proper shower.
When I eat I feel sick, so I haven't been eating.
I can feel the bones under my breasts and sometimes I wonder
how small I can get and how long it will take for anyone to notice.
Sometimes I forget that feeling lonely has nothing to do with being alone.
Have you stopped asking how I am because you're also afraid of the answer?

II
When I was driving I thought about how easy it would be
to just drive over the edge of the road, down the mountain,
and I couldn't understand why this didn't happen all the time.
What is it that keeps us within the yellow lines?

III
We haven't had sex in a while and I know you've noticed,
but don't want to say anything
because you don't want me to feel bad.
I'm not sure why I don't want any part of you
inside any part of me.
Maybe I'm afraid that if you feel inside you'll know how hollow

I have become.
Maybe I'm afraid you'll rattle inside of me
and we'll both get lost in my echoes.
I don't want tongue kisses
and I don't want to go down on you like I used to.
Maybe I'm scared that if you get too close you'll catch it.

CAITLIN SPRING

OVER THE LINE

The dog had destroyed the Christmas decorations.
Knocked over the tree and then ravaged its fruits:
The three wise men, purchased in Hong Kong
on our way back to South Africa from the United States,
the kangaroo from Australia,
the angel and the cross.
There is a lesson here. You said.
I don't want to buy more things. Things can break.
And it is just too painful when they do. I just want to use
up the things I have.
I don't want any more.
I nodded from the other end of the call.
Making occasional sounds so you knew the line hadn't
broken too. I was sad the Christmas decorations I'd known
my whole life were gone.
I was sad you had to mourn the loss of these objects and
their memories.
But things break, Mom. I said. And it is okay to be sad. I
think you're on mourning overload. And adding one more
loss is just too many.
We went back to talking about Mommom. About the
morphine and the diapers.
I'm feeling stronger mentally though. You said.
That's good, Mom. I feel like I'm in a good position to be
here for you.
I'm sorry I cry every time I talk to you. You said.
That's okay. That's why I called.

                                        CAITLIN SPRING

SPOOKASEM
Afrikaans

apart from the man who stole my packet of Pringles and tried to rape me,
I haven't had any bad luck or unfortunate experiences in Thailand.

I
het jy die woord 'spookasem' al ooit handeviervoet
bekruip en opgetel
voor hy teë kon praat op jou rug gaan lê en die woord soos
'n koffietafel
of kat bo jou kop vasgehou elke sentimeter van sy maag
bestudeer
byna versmoor toe hy Raka op jou gesig
kom lê 'n mynskag van jou keel maak
en jou asem in armsvol by sy mond instop

wees rustig – haal net asem
suiker is nie 'n swart dier nie en
'n woord is nie 'n ding wat jou dood kan maak nie maar
spóókasem
wat dóén jy in hierdie wêreld? jy is dood
jy haal nie asem nie – wat is spookasem anders as ek:
'n pastelkleurige wolk wat ineenkrimp en
verdwyn wanneer hande om my vou ek is nou weg maar
ek sal jou nie laat vergeet nie ek sal taai aan jou vel bly
kleef
wanneer jy jou hande teen mekaar vryf sal ek in stukkies
tussen jou vingers uitkruip
ek sal jou nie laat vergeet dat jy my laat verdamp het nie

II
Hua Hin is die mooiste plek wat ek nog gesien het
sy het gegee en gegee en gegee sy het
my nuwe rok soos 'n gulsige kind van my lyf af geruk sy het
baie meer gevat as my pakkie Pringles

III
as ek kon het het ek my vel soos geskenkpapier van my lyf af geskeur as ek kon
het ek myself in 'n asbak doodgedruk soos 'n sigaret trek hy aan my gooi my
as sonder seremonie in die straat waar 'n hond aan my kom ruik
voor ek in palms uit die teer begin groei sien ek 'n laaste keer
gebarste lippe wat in swart branders oor donker gevlekte tande terugtrek

onder my vel het ek niemand ingenooi nie
ek wil net weer op Hua Hin se melkerige seesand sit
ek wil myself in groen blare toedraai waar daai vuil hande my nie kan beetkry my in vuurmaakhout
kleiner kleiner kap my skelet is my houthuis en in haar

sal ek nooit weer alleen wees nie

ELODI TROSKIE

CANDY FLOSS

apart from the man who stole my packet of Pringles and tried to rape me,
I haven't had any bad luck or unfortunate experiences in Thailand.

I
have you ever crept up on the word 'spookasem' on all fours picked it up
before it could talk back lain down on your back holding the word like a coffee table
or cat above your head examining each centimetre of its belly
almost strangled it when it came to lie Raka[1] on your face
made a mineshaft of your throat
shoved armfuls of your breath into its mouth

be calm – just breathe
sugar is not a black animal and
a word is not a thing that can murder you but *spookasem*
what are you doing in this world? you are dead
you are not breathing – I am nothing but *spookasem*:
a pastel-coloured cloud that shrinks and
disappears when hands fold around me I'm gone now but
I won't let you forget I will keep on clinging stickily to your skin
when you rub your hands together I will crawl out in pieces between your fingers
I won't let you forget that you made me evaporate

---

1 Raka refers to the mythical animal in NP van Wyk Louw's eponymous epic poem

II
Hua Hin is the most beautiful place I've seen
she gave and gave and gave she
ripped my new dress off like a greedy child she took
much more than a packet of Pringles

III
if I could I would tear my skin like gift-wrapping from my
body if I could
I would extinguish myself in an ashtray like a cigarette he
pulls me throws my
ash unceremoniously on the street where a dog comes to
sniff at me
before I grow out in palms from the tar I see for the last
time
burst lips that pull back in black waves over dark stained
teeth

I didn't invite anyone in under my skin
I just want to sit on Hua Hin's milky-white sand again
I want to wrap myself in green leaves where those dirty
hands
can't get hold of me to chop me into firewood
smaller and smaller my skeleton is my timber house and in
her

I'll never be alone again

Translated from the Afrikaans original – Elodi Troskie's
Spookasem – *by Pieter Odendaal*

MMILENG WA HILLBROW
Sesotho

Mehoo e ne e le e meholo
Lerata e le le hlohlontshang ditsebe
Setjhaba e le se fetang sa phupu ya letona
Ngwana motho e motsho ba mo kentse taere ya lebidi la koloi molaleng
Ba entse sedikadikwe ba mmokanetse,

Mantswe e le a reng; 'mmolayeng'
'Mmolayeng ke leshodu wa utswa'
'Motjheseng le moqetele'
'Ke moleko o re lekile'

Badumedi ba di etelletse pele ditaba
Ba lebetse ka modimo
Le Beibele ba lebetse ka yona
Ho se mosamaria ya molemo
Lentswe le le leng
Ho tshwere dikwakwa le marumo
Ngwana motho e motsho ba mo tlepenya ka majwe
Ba mo tshela ka peterolo
Madi a mo kwahetse sefahleho,

Ya sebete ke ya neng a tshwere tlobana ya mollo
Le hona o sebete sa ho beha tau setswetse
Menwana ya satalla ya kgomarela tlobana ya mollo
Ya re ha e arohana lelakabe la kwenya setopo se phelang,

Ha e le dihele tsona di hona mona lefatsheng
Kahlolo ha e sa le ya modimo
Le motho wa lefatshe o se a ikahlolela

Ka monahano wa hore ena o tswetse manyeloi
Kapa o tla tswala manyeloi
Bana ba hae e tlo ba manyeloi
Mme ba ke ke ba etsa sebe le ha e le se le seng.

                                                THABANG TSOLO

ON A HILLBROW STREET

The shouting was loud
Ear-piercing noise filled the air
The crowd larger than the funeral of a king
They put a tyre around the neck of the poor African child
Having encircled and cornered him

Voices were saying, 'kill him, kill him!'
'Kill him, he's a thief'
'Burn him to ashes'
He's nothing but trouble

At the forefront were believers
Having forgotten about god
Let alone a Bible
There was no Good Samaritan
Only one voice prevails
They hold spears and matchboxes
With stones they crush the poor child
They pour petrol on him
His face covered in blood

The brave one is he holding a burning torch
His bravery can put a lion to shame
His fingers folded and grabbed the torch
When he unfolded it, flames licked a living body

This is hell on earth
Judgement is no longer for the Lord
Even earthy beings carry it out
With a thought that he has given birth to angels

Or he will give birth to angels
His children will be angels
And they will not commit a single sin

Translated from the Sesotho original – Thabang Tsolo's
Mmileng Wa Hillbrow – *by Goodenough Mashego*

LUFA SIJONGILE!
Xhosa

Ncwadi lwemveli yintoni isikhwasilima mfondini?
Inkal' ixing'etyni kwicala lakho, sekutheni?
Bakhal'esomfazi bayangqukruleka banesingqala abathandi bakho.
Amaqhwa ayakuxovula okwesithungu, akufuna kwesimnyama.
Iinzingo zikupheka zikophula xakunamhlanje.
Uphuhliso likufulathele okwethamsanqa.
Abathandi bakho sebexeli'zinja zabakhwetha ukushiywa enyanyeniGoqo, golokoqo ziyawa iincwadi zababhali bakho kukuvinjwa inkxaso.
Gwalakaxa, ayavalwa amacandelo akho, inkxaso yemali ifulathele.
Kubanda okwempumlo yenja ukuthengwa kweencwadi zakho.
Ncwadi lwemveli ungabisabhubha mfondini ndiyakujoka.
Abasakhulayo badikwe yeyokosa, kaloku bawexulwe zezikaphoyiyana zasemzini.
Iintsizana zabathandi bakho ziyangcokocha.
Zigungquza esithokothokweni sobumnyama, bambalwa abazicingayo.
Ophumeleleyo kunani ukujonga emva ancede abanye.
Lowo uphumileyo ehlathini ufulathel'okwethamsanqa.
Lowo ufuman'amathuba, wenzela yena yedwa.
Kanti ke baziinkambi ezakukuswela ngabo bangafumani kwa iphunga lophuhliso.
Ncwadi lwemveli, sikhule ngawe nakubeni usifa xakunamhlanje.
Hanewu! Boohlohlesakhe luyafa olwemveli zibe neelwimi zomgquba zirhoxoza.

Lusifa nje luyekelwa kwasithi kuba sigcagce nezasemzini.
Namhla xa uthetha nomntwana ngolwenkobe uv'sesithi 'daddy likes to speak in that language', Uzive ngath'uhlatywa ngentsengece entliziyweni.
Wakukhalima akubinze ngombuzo othi 'how is Xhosa going to help me in future', hayike ndincame okwenj'incam'icuba.
Ziphi izidweshane zidwangube zeelwimi zakwantu madoda?
Baphi abathandi boncwadi lwemveli neelwimi zakwantu?
Lowo ufuman' amathuba wenzela okwakhe ukuxhamla, Omny' adazingele amathuba wokwaziwa ezidumisa yena.
Baziingxwelerha ezantsi abathandi boncwadi lwemveli neelwimi zomgqubaNdiva iincwina zabo ezilusizi zisithi, yhini, yhini ukulahlwa kwezasekhaya.
Nxayiphi kwakusithiwa umbona umnandi ngokuchubelana?
Kwakusakuthiwa umntu ngumntu ngabantu.
Kwimizana esihlangana kuyo njengababhali abangathath'intweni, ufika iziindandalazisa zodandatheko,
Kwabanye ikukuncama okukhatshwa ziinzingo.
Abanye bebuza, iphi imizi ebekelwe ukuphuhlisa ezakwantu?
Kunani nokuba inye impendulo, kuloomibuzo ixhaxha ityumze intliziyo.
Nabakhulu wova xa bethetha becezela kude neelwiimi zenkobe nakube nikhule ngazo kephofu.
Ongasentla wasinika ngenjongo ezilwimi engapuci, Akaphindanga wathi ebedlala ngokusinika zona, xa kunamhlanje siyazifulathela.
Ncwadi lwemveli vuka mfondini, chacha ude wenze owenkawu umtsi.
Mhla womelela sizakuvuya sithi tata lahote yathwas'inyanga.
Mhla wahlonitshwa ngokupheleleyo sakuthi sixhelelw'

exhukwana.
Okwangoku usaqhothoza okomkhuhlane wexhego, Ithemba lelokuba umzi ontsundu akayikukuyekela.

Nakubeni okwalomzuzwana useyindoda ebuthathaka, Kodwa liyeza ixesha lokukhonya kwakho, njengendoda yokuqala eAfrika.

Awusokuze ubalelwe kwelabafileyo ncwadi lwemveli.

Zingasokuze zeyele emgxobhozweni iilwimi zakwantu Uncwadi lwemveli ngumthomb' odidi, masibeni yimbumba mawethu!

ATHINI WATU

IT DIES IN OUR WATCH!

Indigenous literatures, what is this crash, man?
You are stuck in a difficult situation on your side, what went wrong?
Your fans cry like women with long cries.
Struggles will press you like a sheaf, when he seeks in darkness.
With grief tossing and turning you to this day.
Development has turned its back on you like luck.
You have abandoned your fans like initiate dogs.
Your writers' books fall from being deprived support.
Your sections are being closed, financial support has turned is back.
Cold as a dog's nose is your book sales.
Indigenous books do not die, man – I plead with you.
The ones growing are extremely annoyed, because they have been lured by foreign foolishness.
Your poor fans are suffering.
They limitedly move within deep darkness, and a few only think of them.
Why can't the successful ones look back and help the others?
The one who has escaped the jungle has turned their back like luck.
The one who has opportunities is doing it only for himself.
Even though they are herds that will be protected by those who don't even experience the slightest of development.
Indigenous literature, you have helped us grow though you are dying today.
Hold on! The indigenous is dying at the same time as indigenous languages are suffering.

It dies because we have neglected it because we have become familiar with the foreign.

Today when you speak to a child in the indigenous language you hear them say, 'Daddy likes to speak in that language.' You feel as though you are being stabbed with a sharp weapon in the heart.

When you sigh he shouts at you with a question: 'How is Xhosa going to help me in the future?', but I give up on the impossible (but I give up like a dog giving up on tobacco).

Where are the shortcuts the nobles of indigenous languages, man?

Where are the lovers of indigenous literature and languages? The one getting opportunities does so for their own benefit. Another would hunt for opportunities to be known in praising themselves.

Lovers of indigenous literature and languages are victims at the bottom.

I hear their sad cries saying, oh why the loss of our indigenous values.

When was it when they said things are enjoyed when sharing?

They used to say a person becomes someone because of someone else.

In the houses that we meet as writers who have nothing, information on stresses,

To others it was giving up accompanied by troubles.

Others asking, where are the houses set aside for developing the indigenous writings.

At least one answer, from those questions that destroy the heart.

Even the greats, you will hear the speaking far from their indigenous languages though you grew up using them.

The One above intentionally gave us these languages without doubt,

He never turned and said he was playing when he gave them to us, but today we turn our backs on them.

Indigenous literature, wake up man, recover to your greatest stride.

The day you find your strength we will rejoice and say finally the day has arrived.

The day you get your unreserved respect we will finally be at home.

For now you are still very frail, like an old man,

Hoping that African people won't give up and let you go.

Even though for now you are still a frail man, but your time to reign will come, as the first man in Africa

You will never be counted among the dead, indigenous literature.

And indigenous languages will never become part of garbage. Indigenous literature is of great stature, let us unite Africans.

Translated from the Xhosa original – Athini Watu's Lufa Sijongile! – *by Innocentia Mhlambi*

LESSONS

My grandmother's hands are wrinkled by time.
Her youth lay buried beneath the calluses and
often peeks through Henna-dipped nails.
The frog in her throat has grown into a giant toad
whose croaking and wheezing have swallowed her laughter

Laughter that faded from her eyes the day my father returned
with my grandfather's hat in a shoebox.

My grandmother whispers secrets to the wind
in a language her children no longer speak.
She sniffs the air and knows when the rains will come,
when the trees will bare fruits;
Her imphepho smoke shows her when the fire
in belly of the rebels will erupt.
Our home is the fifth dwelling she's built between three
countries, across two continents.

My grandmother has crossed many borders with nine children:
'Replace your toothbrush with a pair of pliers;
Braid your hair so you won't need a comb;
Remember to pack your grandfather's pocket knife instead
of a nail file. Beauty is extra baggage that you cannot
afford to pack.'

These items she hands down as we escape home after home.
I want to tell her that these tools cannot break down human borders,
But she has already wrapped her dreams for me between old habits and lost memories,
Hoping that this time they are light enough to carry all the way.

                        FLOW WELLINGTON

MY OUPA'S WATCH

My oupa only wore his watch to church
so that in the middle of talks with the men
he could pull up his sleeve
and pretend to look at the time.
Jammer pastoor, I imagine him saying,
my vrou wag vir my byrie huis.

He was the kind of man
who liked to spend his time at home.
He would take off his watch just before lunch,
placing it neatly on his bedside table.
Unlike ouma who yanks hers off
as if someone is robbing her.

Now that oupa is gone I stare at his watch,
not to tell the time, but to see the minute hand tick.

STEPHANIE WILLIAMS

SEA, BOY

hey kira-kira boy,
hey surf boy,
boy with ocean lung:
Wooh, wooh!

with body of brown you boy the boat,
skin and salt – this is all you know:
warm water, sea snake, wild wave.

you have never sat at a ruler-scratched desk,
and i hope you do.
and i hope you never do

you have never felt the floor of a foreign land,
and i hope you do,
and i hope you never do.

i hope you learn to know the faces, spaces, traces of the world,
and i hope you never do.

oh kira-kira boy,
oh sea scrap boy,

i hope all you ever see is reef, deep and blue.

oh beach-bound boy;

go away boy,
stay boy
grow boy,
bide boy

you are free with the sea
you are jailed with the sea.

BEATRICE WILLOUGHBY

ON THE EDGE OF DARKNESS

We live on the edge of darkness,
accustomed to the brooding veld,
abraded aloes, pellets of kudu,
hills that are sliced into silence.

This deepening shelf of place:
a cave become a den for brown
hyenas. When it's cold at night,
we hear their echoing shrieks

(the stars bleed out, as if they've been
half-chewed by them). We stay alert
for other signs: bones and ash,
tokens of language, fallen leaves.

                        FIONA ZERBST

DISMANTLING FRANKENSTEIN'S MONSTER

When the odds were stacked against us we added 0s and 1s to even out the playing field. By now, binaries gave names that correlated with constituent parts. The nuts and bolts of this body tightened their agenda and we were gendered accordingly. I became a mirror with four hands. The two on top worked tirelessly to remove my feathers one by one and stitched together a shell made out of recycled materials. I was now deflowered and could no longer fly. The bottom two however found each other and I learned to curtsy. There was a method to this madness. My left leg was a lock and my right was a key, bringing them close together would lead to more rapid breakdown. I was already in pieces but gave a hand to the man who needed it. This sacrifice cost me perfect symmetry so an arm and a leg also had to give.
Without this fraction of my body parts I became a key with two hands. Half of a man, or half of a woman but never truly complete. When my eyes finally opened my feathers had become ash. With my index finger I inscribed two words from opposite sides of my cortex and within minutes I completely rewrote their agenda. Now I stand firmly in their midst, without a gender.

                                    THANDIWE ZHANJE

BIOGRAPHIES

Zukiswa Muriel Adonis
Zukiswa Muriel Adonis loves art, going to watch drama performances, travelling and window shopping. She spends most of free time going to flea markets, museums and galleries, and book stores, libraries and lounges to read books, watching cultural dance group performances, and writing poems in vernacular.

Jayne Bauling
Jayne Bauling's short stories and poems have been published in a number of anthologies and literary journals. She is best known for her YA novels which have been awarded several prizes, and two of which are DBE-prescribed high school set-works, while *Dreaming of Light* was chosen to represent South Africa on the 2014 IBBY Honour List. She regularly writes stories for FunDza Literacy Trust, and lives in Mpumalanga.

Michèle Betty
Michèle Betty is the poetry editor of *New Contrast: The South African Literary Journal* and the founder of Dryad Press (Pty) Ltd, an independent press dedicated to the promotion and publication of poetry in South Africa. She has a BA LLB from the University of the Witwatersrand in Johannesburg and an MA in Creative Writing from the University of Cape Town. Her poems have appeared in journals both in South Africa and abroad and have been anthologised in *The Live Canon International Poetry Competition Anthology*, *The Sol Plaatje European Union Anthology* and most recently in *The New Century of South*

African Poetry (Jonathan Ball, 2018). Her debut collection, *Metaphysical Balm*, was published in March 2017 and was shortlisted for the 2018 Ingrid Jonker Prize.

Marike Beyers
Marike Beyers lives, writes and works in Makhanda. Her poems have appeared in South African journals such as *New Coin*, *New Contrast* and *& Stanzas* and some anthologies. Occasionally she reviews books as well. She is the author of two collections of poems, *On Another Page* (Aerial Publishing) and *How to Open the Door* (Modjaji Books).

Nicola Brighton
Nikki Brighton is an activist, writer and enthusiastic contributor to the creative, conscious community in the Midlands of KwaZulu-Natal. She celebrates the small stuff, forages for wild food and walks a lot with her African dog.

Nikki's favourite evening of the month is the small gathering of poets at Steampunk Coffee between the trading store and railway tracks in Lion's River. Here, farmers, artists, teachers, cooks, gardeners and accountants share their poems and observe the unique flavour of the Midlands flourish.

Christine Coates
Christine Coates, a poet and writer from Cape Town, holds an MA in Creative Writing from the University of Cape Town. Her poems and stories have been published in various local and international literary journals. She has two collections of poetry. Her debut collection, *Homegrown* (Modjaji Books, 2014), received an honourable mention

from the Glenna Luschei Prize. Her second collection, *Fire Drought Water*, was published by Damselfly Press in 2018. Christine's poems have been selected for previous *EU Sol Plaatje Poetry anthologies*, *Coming Home: Poems of the Grahamstown Diaspora 2019*, *"New" African Poets Anthologies 2015–2017* and the *Cambridge Conference of Contemporary Poetry Review: Africa Focus*.

Sannah Cujane

Sannah Cujane lives in Verdwaal village in North West province. She is 17 years old and will be matriculating from Regolotswe High School this year.

Luthando Dlamini

Luthando Dlamini was born in Margate, KwaZulu-Natal. He is an information systems student at the University of Cape Town. He was longlisted for the Sol Plaatje European Union Poetry Award in 2016 and 2018.

Chris Ellis

Chris Ellis is a general medical practitioner and author. He writes both humorous and serious articles for medical journals, travel and leisure magazines. His work was selected for the anthology, *Laugh the Beloved Country: The Best of South African Humour of the last 200 Years*.

Kimberly Flanagan

Kimberly Flanagan is a 27-year-old, who resides in Johannesburg with her mother and two children. Kimberly works as a producer for ENCA. She started writing in journals before she started high school and was part of her high school newspaper and went on to write for her university newspaper, the *UJ Observer*. A former news anchor on *Sunrise* breakfast show on etv, she loves reading, writing, watching movies and spending time with her children. Her hopes to inspire people by telling raw and honest stories.

Tshepo Gaerupe

Tshepo Gaerupe is motivational speaker, poet, writer and content creator. He was born and raised in Ganyesa, North West province. Radio presenter at Revival FM, his work has appeared in various publications and online platforms. He is passionate about youth development and language. In October 2017 he won the SOMAFCO UHURU initiative educational tour to Tanzania for writing a winning essay about the role of arts and culture in reducing unemployment in Africa. Tshepo has worked with various organisations in the arts and creative industry such as JT Communications, Badilisha X-Change and Avbob Poetry Anthology.

Dawn Garisch

Dawn Garisch has had seven novels, a collection of poetry, short stories, a non-fiction work and a memoir published. She has had five plays and short film produced, and has written for television. Three of her novels have been published in the UK.

Her novel, *Accident*, was long-listed for the Barry Ronge Sunday Times fiction award. Karavan Press recently published her latest novel *Breaking Milk*. Her latest collection of poetry titled *Disturbance* will come out from Modjaji Books shortly.

She is a founding member of the Life Righting Collective (https://www.liferighting.com/). She teaches memoir writing, is a medical doctor and lives in Cape Town.

Sarah Godsell
Sarah Godsell is a historian, poet and teacher. She is passionate about being brave about uncovering our history to face our present and future. She has published two collections of poetry, *Seaweed Sky* (Poetree Publications, 2016) and *Liquid Bones* (Impepho Press, 2018).

Vernon R.L. Head
Head is author of a *Tree For the Birds*, *The Search for the Rarest Bird in the World* and a poetry collection called *The Laughing Dove and Other Poems*. He watches the natural world inquiringly and he is waiting to find windows in walls.

Miyelani Anthonia Hlungwani
Born in 1989, Miyelani Anthonia Hlungwani grew up in Mukhomi village, outside Malamulele in Limpopo. In 2007, he passed his matric with a merit. Then, in 2008, he went to the University of Venda, where he enrolled for a Bachelor of Arts degree (Media and Language Studies) . In 2010, he was awarded a Certificate of Participation in Xitsonga Linguistic Fieldwork from Central Connecticut State University (USA). He self-published a Xitsonga anthology titled, *Hi le misaveni*, as an e-book. In 2018, he was awarded a certificate to work as a mentor for WritePublishRead programme by Via Afrika Publishers, in partnership with the NRF and SARChI Research Chair in the field of Intellectualisation of African Languages, Multilingualism and Education (NRF Chair in African Languages) and the African Language Association of Southern Africa (ALASA). This year, he completed a BA(Hons) in African Languages from UNISA.

Mashimbye Owners Hluvukani
Mashimbye Owners Hluvukani is an award-winning poet. A BCom graduate and an educator by profession, he's currently pursuing his career in account management at a power utility company. He developed his love for poetry and writing while he was still in primary school.

Alice Inggs
Alice Inggs is a writer and editor from South Africa. She has an MA from the University of Cape Town. Alice has contributed to a number of publications, including *Asymptote*, *The Arkansas International*, *EuropeNow*, *Critical Arts*, *Ons Klyntji*, *VICE* and *Rolling Stone*.

Siphelele Khaphetshu
Siphelele Khaphetshu is a Xhosa poetess, born in Queenstown in the Eastern Cape. She is currently based in Bloemfontein, studying at the University of the Free State. Siphelele is a very cultural person and she embraces different cultures. Her stage name is Intombi yomXhosa.

Zandile Khumalo
Zandile Khumalo writes poetry, short stories and is currently working on a Zulu novel. It will be her first and will be published later in 2019.

Zamokwakhe Kumbe
Zamokwakhe, also known as Mrs Write, spends most of her time reading, researching and designing cool stuff with her gifted hands. When she's not thinking of her next creative endeavour, you can find her amassing inspiration from nature. She has worked as a copywriter for reputable advertising agencies and is now working on

her second poetry anthology. PS. She is also a closet rapper.

Sarah Lubala
Sarah Lubala is a Congolese-born South African writer. She has been shortlisted for the Gerald Kraak Award and The Brittle Paper Poetry Award. Her work has been published in *Brittle Paper*, *The Missing Slate*, *Apogee Journal*, *The Shallow Ends* as well as The Gerald Kraak anthologies, *As You Like It* and *The Heart of the Matter*, Botsoso's *2018 Poetry from Public and Private Places* and the African Collective's *Best New African Poets 2018 Anthology*.

Zamokuhle Madinana
Zama Madinana is a Johannesburg-based poet. He holds a BCompt degree from The University of South Africa. His poems have been published in *Stanzas*, *Botsotso*, *Carapace* and other literary journals. In 2016, he published his collection of poems, *A Womb of Time*.

Afikile Madiya
21-year-old Afikile Madiya is from the Eastern Cape province, who has studied digital marketing. She is passionate about religion and education-related issues. She is also a volunteer for organisations that fight for the wellbeing of women.

Clare Manicom
Clare has always loved words, stories and music. Poetry has become a comfortable home for her to share her experiences of her world. She lives in Cape Town and is part of a women's poetry group, the Creative Sisterhood, which participated in the McGregor Poetry Festival in 2018 and

in 2019. She has retired from formal employment to live a more balanced life.

Ayanda Masango
Ayanda Masango is a Ndebele poet and writer, who lives in Mpumalanga province. She has been very inspired by literature, especially poetry and novels, since childhood. She is currently pursing a diploma in journalism at Rosebank College.

Bongani Masilela
Bongani Masilela is a native of Middelburg. He is a poet, mathematician, human rights activist and has international banking experience and qualification. Masilela has authored a poetry anthology titled, *Then I Don't Want to be a Poet*. He writes in three South African languages and some of his work has been published in Austria, Ghana and Japan. Some of Masilela's Haiku has been translated to German in Austria. His isiNdebele poem, 'Ngiyanilibalela', was published in the *The Sol Plaatje European Union Poetry Anthology Volume VIII*.

Linda Masilela
Linda Masilela is a medical student and a poet in his spare time. He uses poetry as a medium to try and understand the world and question the current status quo. He has performed at Current State of Poetry, Word and Sound, Tshwane Speak Out Loud and Wits Poets Corner. With his poetry, he hopes to reach out to more audiences and write a book in the near future.

Aaron Mpho Masowa
Aaron Mpho Masowa is the writer with Master's degree in

African Languages and is currently registered for a PhD at University of the Free State. He has written four books.

Tebogo Matshana
Tebogo Boikanyo Matshana is a visual artist and writer based in Johannesburg. She attained a Bachelor of Fine Art through Rhodes University in 2018. Her love for story-telling emerged as a child, when she would express herself creatively through short stories, poems and illustrations. Her passion for story-telling bloomed into her career and now manifests most prevalently in her love for children's story writing, illustration and 2D animation.

Mzoli Mavimbela
Mzoli Mavimbela is a social worker by profession. He is a poet and an Xhosa indie author. Originally from Port St John's, Eastern Cape, he currently resides in George, Western Cape, where he is doing his Master's degree in Social Work (Research) at Nelson Mandela University. He has published various poems at www.avbobpoetry.co.za. Reading books is his hobby.

Jeannie Wallace McKeown
Jeannie Wallace McKeown lives in Grahamstown and works full-time at Rhodes University. She has an MA in Creative Writing from Rhodes, and has had poems published in *New Coin*, *New Contrast*, *Poetry Potion*, *Aerodrome* and other literary journals. Her work appears in the anthologies *Voices Of This Land* 2nd Edition, *For Rhino in a Shrinking World*, the *EU Sol Plaatjie anthologies VI and VII*, and on the AVBOB Poetry website. Her collection, *Unremembered Poems*, will be published by Modjaji Books in 2019.

Frank Meintjies
Based in Johannesburg, Frank Meintjies works in the field of social development. Frank's creative writing has been included in several South African anthologies. He also contributes to the world of poetry through participation in public readings. Frank's most recent poetry collection *is Unfettered Days* and he has written several short stories. In his writing, he explores issues such as identity, community and social change.

Janine Milne
Janine Milne holds a Bachelor's degree in Theory of Literature and Creative Writing with distinctions, from the University of South Africa. Janine won the McGregor Poetry festival poetry competition 2017 and was a finalist in the same contest in 2018. Janine has had several poems published in the *Sol Plaatje Award Anthology, volumes IV and VIII*. Her short stories were chosen for the coveted *Short Sharp Stories Anthology*, *Die Laughing* and *The Bloody Parchment – the South African Horror Festival anthology 2016*. She is currently working on her first poetry collection and novel.

Matete Motsoaledi
Matete is a Sepedi writer and performer whose work has appeared in poetry collections around South Africa. He is among the indigenous language activists who seek to preserve language by creating modern literary work and fusing literature with other artforms.

Zimkitha Mpatheni
Zimkitha, a young Xhosa girl, was raised in Stellenbosch. She pursued a BA degree in International Studies at the

University of Stellenbosch, and further got a Masters in Applied Linguistics and TESOL from Portsmouth University, UK. She studied linguistics due to her interest in how languages can shape societies and provide a connection with the rest of the world, especially in literature and poetry. She has taught in Turkey, Saudi Arabia and now northern Iraq for 10 years, which have inspired her to write about her experiences as South African in the Middle East.

Kwazi Ndlangisa
Kwazi Ndlangisa, an executive director and founder of Pot Of Art is a multi-award-winning performance poet from South Africa, a writer, facilitator and arts events curator rooted in the deep rural areas of UMzimkhulu called Chamto, KwaBhaca on the South Coast of KwaZulu-Natal.

Abongile Njamela
Abongile Njamela, best known by his stage name 'Abospitter', is a rapper, poet and actor from Khayelitsha. He began his poetry journey in 2017 where he won the Word N Sound King Of The Mic. He is now the current Prim Poetry Champ & the Western Cape Provincial slam champion and will participate in the National Slam organised by CSP late this year.

Zukisani Nongogo
Zola Nongogo was born in the Eastern Cape in Mount Ayliff and currently lives in Cape Town. He has been published in *The Sol Plaatje European Union Poetry Anthology 2015, 2017, 2018* and the online literary journal *Eunoia Review* under the name Zukisani Nongogo.

Fumane Ntlhabane

Fumane Ntlhabane is a Johannesburg-based South African poet, writer, presenter and radio personality. She is inspired by the strength that lies in the human form and often writes about her experiences in the body of a black woman in society. She began her journey in the arts with CSP in 2017 where she went on to participate in the Gauteng provincial slam, where she placed in the top 5. She has performed on many stages in and around Johannesburg including being invited as a performer for the 2019 Human Rights Festival, where she shared a stage with esteemed poets such as Vangi Gansho, Lebogang Mashile and Napo Mashiane. Fumane is also a co-author of a book titled *Colour Me Melanin*, which is a colouring book accompanied by praise poetry that teaches self-love to the young African women.

Thulani Ntisana

Thulani Ntisana is currently registered as a Master's student in the department of sociology at Rhodes University. He completed his undergraduate degree in Social Science, majoring in sociology and psychology from the University of Fort Hare and his Bachelor of Social Science (Hons) (BSSH) from Rhodes. He was born in a small town of Dutywa, Eastern Cape, South Africa. He grew up in Nqamakwe and Butterworth, and currently resides in Grahamstown.

Sihle Ntuli

Sihle Ntuli is a Kwa-Mashu-born South African writer with an MA from the School of Languages and Literature at Rhodes University. He is a former lecturer of classical civilisations at the University of the Free State where he was a recipient of the 2019 Innovation Award for Curriculum

Design and Delivery. Since 2009, his poems have been published in *New Coin*, *New Contrast*, *Itch* and *Saraba*, amongst others. He has also been published in an array of African anthologies such as the *Best New African Poets 2015 Anthology* and the *Sol Plaatjie EU Poetry Anthology in 2016 & 2017*.

Mushayathoni Nwovhe
Mushayathoni Bridget Nwovhe is a medical student. In 2017, she published a poetry collection titled, *Calendar's Time*. Her work has appeared in *Fundza*, *AVBOB Poetry*, *Kalahari Review*, *The New Ink Review* and *Empowered* youth magazine. She was a finalist of the 2018 Sol Plaatje European Union Poetry Award. She is also featured in the poetry anthology titled, *Tapping into Poetry*.

Zukiswa Pakama
Zukiswa Pakama has a degree in journalism and is a published author of children's books in Xhosa. *Akulahlwa Mbeleko Ngakufelwa* won the Maskew Miller Literature Award and the IBBY Honour in 2018. Another book, *Saphela isizungu kuZingi*, got an award in 2017. She also writes scripts for TV shows and is currently teaching isiXhosa at Jan van Riebeeck primary school.

Kagiso Mosima Phakane
Mosima Phakane has won the AVBOB poetry competition in the Sepedi category for 2017 and is working on improving her writing skills at all times. She's part of Poet's Corner, a student society at University of the Witwatersrand, which helps develop poetry skills and ignite the inspiration to keep writing. She writes for love and to motivate and inspire others.

Catherine Pritchard

Pritchard is a journalist by training, creative director and copywriter by trade and poet/traveller/philosopher/photographer by vocation. What connects these and her is story. In 2019, at the formative age of 41, she started a YouTube Channel called "Greater than 40" to bring levity to the gravity of ageing. She is currently working on her first poetry book on ageing while trying to bring rhyme and reason to children's picture books. Making money is a hobby.

Wesley Roodt

Wesley Roodt is a filmmaker and television producer from Port Elizabeth. He works for a television production company and training provider called The Media Workshop, where he writes and directs screen content productions and trains students in television production.

Moses Seletisha

An award-wining Sepedi poet, translator and author of *Tšhutšhumakgala*, Seletisha is from Limpopo. He is the winner of Sol Plaatje EU Poetry Award in 2017, the first poet to win the prize in a language other than English and Afrikaans, for the poem 'Mahlalerwa'. In the same year Seletisha won a prestigious South African literary award as first-time published author. He was published in more than 20 literary journals in South Africa and Africa.

Siwaphiwe Fortune Shweni

Siwaphiwe Fortune Shweni was born in the Eastern Cape and is a graduate of Cape Peninsula University of Technology.

His work is published online by *Kalahari Review*

Magazine and *AVBOB Poetry*. He is also published in the following poetry anthologies – *Voices on Fire* by McGregor Poetry Festival, *Nostalgia* by Prufrock magazine, *I Wish I'd Said* by AVBOB Poetry and *Sol Plaatjie EU Poetry Anthology Vol VIII*.

Caitlin Spring
After completing an Honours degree in Creative Writing at Wits, Caitlin travelled to China for a Master's Degree in International Relations at Peking University. She currently lives in Cape Town, where she eats pizza, works as the content strategist at SnapScan, and sometimes writes poetry.

Elodi Troskie
Elodi Troskie is a 21-year old writer and poet from South Africa, currently living in Bali, Indonesia where she is working as a copywriter. She made her poetry debut in Nuwe Stemme 6 in 2016 and is working on her first solo collection of poems.

Thabang Tsolo
Thabang Tsolo was born in the North West province and writes only in Sesotho. His work has been published in *The Sol Plaatje European Union Poetry Anthology Vol VII*.

Athini Watu
Athini Watu was born in the Eastern Cape province and currently resides in Cape Town. He is the playwright and a poet with a diploma in IT, computer science and data science. He writes because of his love for literature and has a passion for African languages.

Flow Wellington
Flow Wellington is a writer and publisher who lives in Johannesburg. She is the author of two collections, *The Undelivered Score* (2011) and *GauTrained* (2018), both self-published through her own publishing house Poetree Publications. Wellington is a decorated author who has published locally and internationally, has featured on a 2009 Hype Award mixtape and shared stages across the country with musical artists such as Bokani Dyer and Nancy Ginindza. Her company has helped numerous authors publish their writing since 2011, with 21 titles currently recorded.

Stephanie Williams
Stephanie is currently studying towards her Honours degree in English at the University of the Western Cape, with an elective in creative writing. Her literary interests include women's writing and African literature.

Beatrice Willoughby
Beatrice Willoughby is a freelance copywriter from Cape Town. In between her freelance work, forest runs and overseas ventures, she enjoys reading and writing poetry. Her subject matter includes love, life and all things sad, mad and rad (the working title of the collection she one day hopes to publish).

Fiona Zerbst
Fiona Zerbst is the author of four poetry collections to date: *Oleander* (Modjaji Books, 2009), *Time and Again* (UCT Younger Poets Series No 1/Snailpress, 2002), *the small zone* (Snailpress, 1995) and *Parting Shots* (Carrefour Press, 1991). She received an MA in Creative Writing from

the University of Cape Town, studying under the late Stephen Watson, and received a PhD in Creative Writing from the University of Pretoria in 2018 (under the supervision of David Medalie).

Thandiwe Zhanje

Thandiwe Zhanje is an 18-year-old poet and student living in Johannesburg. Her work explores multiple themes including the politics of self, the relationship between present and past, immigration and belonging. She believes that the world can be transformed through the arts and actively inserts her voice in the multitude advocating for a world that speaks in colour and liberation. Thandiwe also teaches Mathematics and Science with the understanding that it is within the giving that the greatest growth occurs. She has great aspirations of exploring her continent and herself through becoming a playwright.

WHAT IS THE EUROPEAN UNION?

The European Union (EU) is a unique economic and political union between 28 European countries[1] that together cover much of the European continent. The EU was created in the aftermath of the Second World War. The first steps were to foster economic cooperation, the idea being that countries that trade with one another become economically interdependent and so more likely to avoid conflict.

Since its birth, the Union has developed into a huge single market with the euro as its common currency. What began as a purely economic union has evolved into an organisation spanning policy areas from climate, environment and health to external relations and security, justice and migration.

The single or 'internal' market is the EU's main economic engine, enabling most goods, services, money and people to move freely. Another key objective is to develop this huge resource also in other areas like energy, knowledge and capital markets to ensure that Europeans can draw the maximum benefit from it.

The EU is based on the rule of law: everything it does is founded on treaties, voluntarily and democratically agreed by its member countries. It actively promotes human rights and democracy and in 2012 was awarded the Nobel Peace Prize for advancing the causes of peace, reconciliation, democracy and human rights in Europe.

---

1. At the time of writing, Belgium, Bulgaria, Croatia, Czech Republic, Denmark, Germany, Estonia, Ireland, Greece, Spain, France, Italy, Cyprus, Latvia, Lithuania, Luxembourg, Hungary, Malta, the Netherlands, Austria, Poland, Portugal, Romania, Slovenia, Slovakia, Finland, Sweden and the United Kingdom.

How does it work?
EU member states have set up institutions to run the EU and adopt its legislation. The main ones are:
- The European Parliament (representing the people of Europe)
- The Council of the European Union (representing national governments)
- The European Commission (representing the common EU interest)

Size and population
The EU is less than half the size of the United States covering some 4 million square kilometres. In terms of size, France is the EU's largest country and Malta its smallest. The EU has a population of close to 505 million people – the world's third largest after China and India.

EU symbols
- The European flag – The 12 stars in a circle symbolise the ideals of unity, solidarity and harmony among the peoples of Europe.
- The European anthem – The melody used to symbolise the EU comes from Ludwig Van Beethoven's 9th Symphony composed in 1823.
- Europe Day – The ideas behind the EU were first put forward on 9 May 1950 by French foreign minister, Robert Schuman. This is why 9 May is celebrated as a key date for the EU.
- The EU motto – "United in diversity".

The EU's economy
Operating as a single market, the EU is a major world trading power. EU economic policy seeks to sustain growth

by investing in transport, energy and research while minimising the impact of further economic development on the environment. Measured in terms of the goods and services it produces, its economy is bigger than that of the US.

The EU and South Africa – a partnership of equals

Since 1994 the growing relationship between South Africa and the EU has been underpinned by the Trade, Development and Cooperation Agreement (TDCA). Closer ties between the two parties were consolidated in 2007 with the establishment of the EU-SA Strategic Partnership. This partnership, the only one of its kind with an African country, is centred on enhanced political dialogue around issues of shared interest including climate change, the global economy, governance, bilateral trade, and peace and security matters. In line with this, its action plan encompasses sectoral cooperation on a range of issues such as climate change, environment, education, science and technology, space, trade and migration. Regular high level meetings steer the partnership, along with the EU-South Africa Joint Cooperation Council. They provide the occasions to discuss current bilateral, regional and global issues.

Trade and investment

The EU is not only South Africa's biggest trading partner but remains the dominant source of foreign direct investment into South Africa (74%). EU-generated investments have created in excess of 500,000 direct jobs. Both South Africa's exports to the EU and imports from the EU are in the region of €24 billion. More importantly, half of South Africa's exports to the EU consist of manufactured goods, which contribute directly to beneficiation and employment and thus to inclusive growth. The entry into force of the SADC-EU Economic Partnership Agreement is generating new opportunities to further strengthen bilateral trade and investment relations.

Development cooperation

The EU remains an important development partner to South Africa, providing significant external assistance funds. The EU's total indicative grant budget for South Africa for the period 2014–20 amounts to some €250 million. It is complemented by a €416 million loan finance envelope from the European Investment Bank (EIB) as well as grant funding from the EU member states.